GREAT ESCAPES

TRUE STORIES

Real Tales of Harrowing Getaways

JUDY DODGE CUMMINGS

This book was manufactured by CGB Printers,
North Mankato, Minnesota, United States
August 2017, Job #228808
ISBN Softcover: 978-1-61930-616-5
ISBN Hardcover: 978-1-61930-612-7

Educational Consultant, Marla Conn

Questions regarding the ordering of this book should be addressed to
Nomad Press
2456 Christian St.
White River Junction, VT 05001
www.nomadpress.net

Printed in the United States.

Contents

Titles in the
Mystery & Mayhem Series

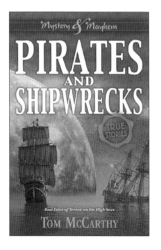

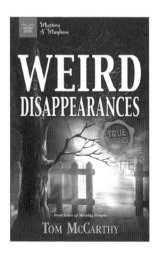

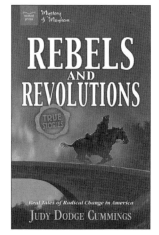

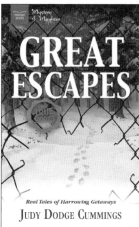

Introduction

Run for Your Life

The door to freedom slams shut and the lock snaps into place. Darkness surrounds you. First, the gloom clouds your vision, then it seeps into your soul. Your heartbeat quickens. Suddenly, you cannot seem to draw enough air into your lungs. You are trapped. Will this prison become your tomb?

But hope is not lost. The glimmer of an escape plan forms in your brain. It will be dangerous, even foolhardy. You have to muster every last ounce of courage and strength. Do you have what it takes to run for your life?

The human spirit craves freedom. When liberty is lost, people go to great lengths to get it back.

In this book, you will read about five ingenious escapes. You'll meet people willing to do whatever it takes to flee their surroundings.

Prisons take many forms. For example, slavery once doomed African American slaves to the lifelong prison of their masters' whims. But in 1848, William and Ellen Craft made a bold dash for freedom. Donning clever disguises, the married couple escaped in broad daylight and fled 1,000 miles.

In another time and place, Douglas Mawson battled a power greater than any human villain. In 1913, Mother Nature trapped him in her icy Antarctic jaws. Alone and dangling by a fraying rope over a bottomless crevasse, all Douglas had to help him escape were his strength and his will to live.

In 1943, Nazi guards packed Belgian Jews into trains headed for Auschwitz, a concentration camp where millions of people were killed. The train cars were so crowded, people had to take turns sitting down. A hunk of moldy bread and a mouthful of water was their only sustenance.

As bad as the train was, 11-year-old Simon Gronowski knew what awaited him at Auschwitz would be worse. He was determined to find a way off the train as it hurtled ever closer to its ghastly destination. How would you escape?

Alcatraz was a rocky prison fortress designed to hold inmates until the end of their sentence or death, whichever came first. Prison officials bragged that it was impossible to escape. But in 1962, three inmates vanished, never to be seen again.

A wall divided the German city of Berlin down the middle for 28 years. This concrete barrier separated families and was closely guarded by communist East German police. East German citizens were not allowed to flee to democratic West Germany. But during two days in 1964, 29 East Germans crawled under the wall in a desperate race for freedom.

These people all faced different kinds of prisons, but they shared common traits. They had guts, grit, skill, and a lot of luck. Keep reading and you may find your pulse quickening as if you, too, were running for your life.

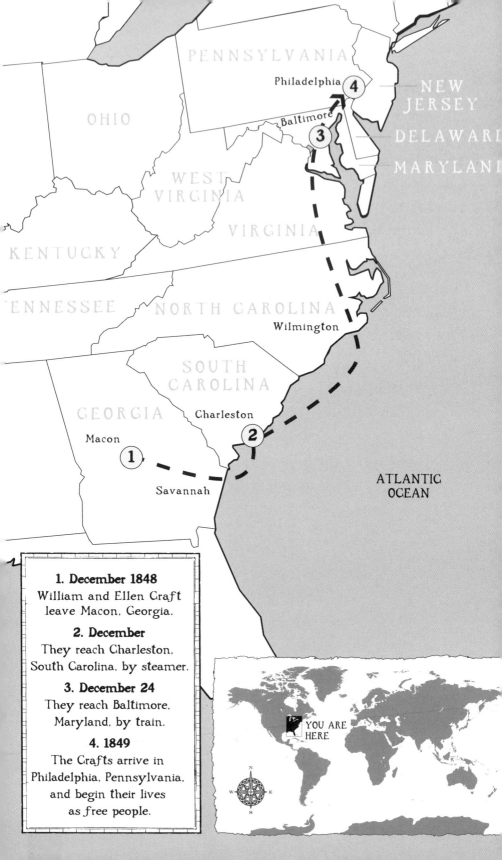

PENNSYLVANIA

Philadelphia ④

NEW JERSEY

OHIO

Baltimore ③

DELAWARE

MARYLAND

WEST VIRGINIA

VIRGINIA

KENTUCKY

TENNESSEE

NORTH CAROLINA

Wilmington

SOUTH CAROLINA

GEORGIA

Charleston

Macon

①

②

ATLANTIC OCEAN

Savannah

1. December 1848
William and Ellen Craft leave Macon, Georgia.

2. December
They reach Charleston, South Carolina, by steamer.

3. December 24
They reach Baltimore, Maryland, by train.

4. 1849
The Crafts arrive in Philadelphia, Pennsylvania, and begin their lives as free people.

YOU ARE HERE

N
W   E
S

| 1619 | | 1848 | 1861 | 1865 |

1619 — The first slaves are brought to the colonies in America

1848 — The Crafts flee the South

1861 — The Civil War begins

1865 — Slavery is abolished

Chapter One

A Thousand Miles

For more than 200 years, slavery was legal in the United States. Punishments for trying to escape were severe. Runaways who were caught were whipped, maimed, or sold.

However, slavery was so awful that tens of thousands of enslaved people took their chances and ran. Most slaves fled in the middle of the night. They hid out in swamps and forests and were chased by bloodhounds. These flights for freedom usually ended in failure.

The story of William and Ellen Craft is different. This couple escaped from slavery in broad daylight and in first-class comfort.

William Craft knew sorrow. Born a slave in Macon, Georgia, in 1824, his parents and brother were sold when William was young. He was left with only his little sister. Then, when he was 16, William lost her, too. Their owner had fallen into debt and decided to sell the two children.

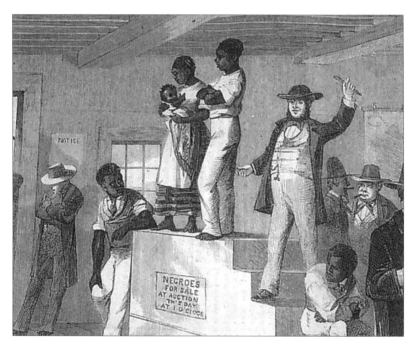

Illustrated London News, England, February 16, 1861

Slave auctions were often held on the steps of the courthouse. As townsfolk strolled past, buyers examined the human wares. The slaves were lined up according to height, and the slave trader ordered them to remove their coats or shawls.

Interested buyers ran their hands over the slaves' bodies, fingering joints and kneading muscles. Slaves kept their faces blank while their mouths were pried open and their gums examined for signs of disease. A slave might be stripped to the waist by buyers looking for scars of whippings. No one wanted to buy a disobedient slave.

Sellers ordered the slaves to jump and dance so buyers could judge their strength and nimbleness.

William might have been spared this humiliation because he was a skilled worker. His owner had apprenticed William to a cabinetmaker, where he learned carpentry. Southern industry was expanding in the early nineteenth century and people needed laborers. Anyone who bought William could make a tidy profit by renting him out.

William's sister was sold first. As her new owner led her away, the auctioneer ordered William to step up on the auction block. But the boy could not take his eyes off his sister. William motioned to a slave friend standing nearby.

"Run and ask the man who bought my sister if he can wait until I am sold," William said, "so I can bid her farewell." The friend ran after the man, but returned a moment later with bad news. The buyer refused to wait.

William turned to the auctioneer and fell to his knees. "Please, sir," he begged. "May I just step down a moment and bid my sister a last farewell?"

The auctioneer grabbed William by the neck and yanked him to his feet. "Get up! . . . there is no use in seeing her."

The bidding began. William looked over the heads of the buyers and watched his sister climb into the back of a cart. She locked eyes with him, tears streaming down her cheeks.

As the cart slowly disappeared into the distance, William's heart swelled with such sadness he thought it might burst.

Two men purchased William—Ira E. Taylor and Robert Collins. Taylor was a bank clerk and Collins was a physician and founder of the Monroe and Bibb Counties Railroad and Banking Company. A wealthy man, Collins owned 1,000 acres of land and 62 slaves, including one young woman named Ellen Smith.

Ellen's mother was a biracial housemaid. Ellen's father was her mother's owner, a wealthy man named James Smith, who had a plantation in Clinton, Georgia. This made Ellen three-quarters white. She was so light-skinned that visitors to the estate often mistook her for a family member.

Mrs. Smith hated Ellen because the girl reminded her of her husband's unfaithfulness. Every day, Ellen became the target of the woman's rage.

Eventually, Mrs. Smith found a way to get rid of Ellen permanently. In 1837, the Smith's daughter, Eliza, married Robert Collins. As a wedding present, Mrs. Smith gave Ellen to Eliza Collins. Although she was only 11 years old, Ellen was taken from her mother and sent to live with Robert Collins and his new wife in Macon, Georgia.

For the rest of her life, Ellen was haunted by memories of how much she had missed her mother while growing up. She never wanted her own children to experience such loss.

Ellen was a personal maid. Petticoats, corsets, hoop skirts, silk, and straw hats consumed her day. She also helped her mistress bathe and dress and kept the bedchamber clean. When Eliza Collins went shopping, Ellen carried bags. She held the umbrella over her owner's head when it rained.

By the standards of slave life, Ellen was privileged. Eliza Collins was kind to Ellen, perhaps because they were half-sisters. While most ladies' maids slept on pallets at the foot of their mistress's beds, Ellen was given a one-room cabin behind the family home. She was never sent to the sugar house, where slaves were whipped or branded as punishment.

But Ellen was still a slave. The law denied her basic rights: to be paid for her work, to travel when and where she wanted, to learn to read, and to be legally married. And, worst of all, if Ellen ever had children, they, too, would be slaves, and could be take away from her at any time.

William Craft and Ellen Smith met at the house of Eliza and Robert Collins.

History is silent about the first time William and Ellen laid eyes on each other, but the moment can be imagined. Perhaps William came to the Collins house to deliver his monthly pay to Mr. Collins. He was walking up the steps of the back porch when the door opened. A slim, young woman stepped out. Her skin was so fair that William assumed she was a member of the Collins family. He lowered his gaze to show proper respect to a white woman.

But then the girl spoke. Maybe she asked his name or what business he had at the house. Soon, William realized that this woman was a slave, too. Just like him.

However it happened, Ellen and William fell in love.

Ira Taylor and Robert Collins rented William out to the cabinetmaker he had been apprenticed to. William was allowed to keep a tiny portion of his pay. Penny by precious penny, he slowly built up savings.

Despite Ellen's special position in the household, the Collinses refused to allow the couple to get married in a church. They did, however, permit William and Ellen to "jump the broom." This was a ceremony enslaved people performed to symbolize a commitment between a man and woman.

Once married, the couple wanted children. However, they remembered the pain of being separated from their parents as children. The Crafts were determined that no child of theirs would be born into slavery. The time had come to escape.

The Underground Railroad was a secret network of anti-slavery activists who aided runaways. These "agents" sheltered fugitives and guided them north. But the Underground Railroad did not exist in the Deep South, and Georgia was in the Deep South. Ellen and William would have to escape on their own.

The couple considered one plan after another. If they simply ran north, slave patrols armed with packs of bloodhounds would follow their scent. They would have to hide in swamps by day and run by night. Macon, Georgia, was more than 800 miles from the free city of Philadelphia, Pennsylvania. The Crafts would be on the run for weeks. Capture was almost guaranteed.

A ship or train could reach Pennsylvania in a few days. But it was illegal for slaves to travel on any public vehicle without a pass from their master.

In December 1848, William came up with a bold plan. Because Ellen was three-quarters white, she was very fair skinned. Although it was not considered proper for a white woman to travel alone, a white *man* could do it. What if, William suggested, Ellen disguised herself as a wealthy white man attended by his slave. They could travel north by train and ship, hiding in plain sight.

Never, insisted Ellen!

She would not be able to fool anyone. Not for a minute, let alone days. They would be caught. The Collinses would send them into the cotton fields or sell them. Such a future was too terrifying to consider.

But Ellen considered the alternative. If they did not try to escape, their future was guaranteed. It would be a life of unending slavery for themselves and any children they had. The thought was unendurable.

"I will do it," Ellen finally said.

She believed God was on their side, so maybe, just maybe, they had a chance.

Their first step was to get passes to be away from work for a few days. This would give the Crafts a head start before anyone knew they were missing. Mrs. Collins was happy to give Ellen a pass. However, when William asked the cabinetmaker for one, the man hesitated.

"It's a busy time of year," he said, eying William suspiciously. It was almost Christmas.

William lowered his gaze and struggled to keep his face blank.

Eventually, the cabinetmaker shrugged. He signed the pass, but reminded William that he had better return by the deadline. Or else.

The next step was Ellen's disguise.

Luckily, William had savings, which he dipped into and used to go shopping. Wary of raising suspicions, he bought each item at a different store. A gentleman's suit coat. A top hat. A pair of glasses with green lenses. While William shopped, Ellen sewed a pair of men's trousers. They hid everything in Ellen's cabin.

Ellen Craft disguised as a white man

The night before the escape, the couple huddled in the cabin. In hushed voices, they went through the plan step by step. Ellen immediately spotted two serious problems. Hotel guests usually had to sign their names in a visitor's register, but Ellen did not know how to write. And Ellen's face was smooth and hairless, not at all like a man's.

"I'll become an invalid," she declared.

William fashioned a sling for her right arm. Now no one could expect her to write. Ellen concocted a poultice for her face and cut a flannel bandage to run under her chin and around her head. Now Ellen's smooth cheeks would be covered.

As the sun came up on the Crafts' last morning in Georgia, Ellen was transformed. William cut her hair short. She put on the suit, bandaged herself up and donned the top hat and glasses. Ellen stood in the center of the cabin and struck a pose. William studied his wife through critical eyes.

"She made a most respectable-looking gentleman," he later said.

For a moment, the two just looked at each other in silence. Then, William took Ellen by the hand and pulled her to the door. He opened it and peeked out. Trees and bushes surrounded the house. Birds sang their morning song. Squirrels and mice rustled the leaves and grass. All was normal.

"My dear," William whispered, "let us make a desperate leap for liberty."

Ellen hesitated. She rested her head against his chest for a long moment and then took a deep breath, steeling herself. "Come, William," Ellen said, lifting her head. "It is getting late . . . let us venture upon our perilous journey."

They walked out the door, taking their first steps on the road to freedom.

William and Ellen took different routes to the train station. William arrived first and sat in the luggage car, where slaves and free blacks were required to ride. Ellen bought two tickets for Savannah, Georgia, about 200 miles away and took a seat in the first-class car. Then they waited.

The train engine rumbled, smoke puffing from its chimney like an iron dragon. People milled about on the train platform. Minutes ticked by as the sun rose higher in the sky. William kept watch out the window, his stomach a spider's nest of nerves.

Suddenly, he saw someone who turned his blood to ice water.

The cabinetmaker stood on the platform talking to the ticket seller. The man had been suspicious when William asked for a pass. Now he was here to track a slave he suspected was making a run for it.

William shrank back into his seat and turned away from the window. Terror filled him and he flinched at every sound. Capture could be seconds away.

The cabinetmaker walked alongside the train, peering into the windows of each car. He glanced in Ellen's compartment. She saw him and shock jolted through her. But the cabinetmaker just glanced over this white man with the bandaged face and walked on. Every second, he drew closer to the car that held William.

Suddenly, the whistle blew and the train began to chug slowly down the tracks. The cabinetmaker had to jump off. The train rolled out of the station and William relaxed at last. They were on their way.

Ellen sighed in relief and turned away from the window. While she had been watching the cabinetmaker, a man had sat down beside her. Now Ellen glanced at him and her breath caught in her throat. Sitting mere inches away was Mr. Crayson, a friend of the Collinses. He had known Ellen since she was a child.

Terrified that Crayson would recognize her voice, Ellen looked out the window again. Crayson said, "Good morning, sir."

Ellen pretended to be deaf and did not turn her head. A minute later, Crayson repeated his greeting, louder this time. Ellen's heartbeat thudded in her ears.

She did not move or speak.

Another passenger in the compartment laughed. Crayson said, "I will make him hear." Then he shouted, "Good morning, sir."

Ellen turned then. She glanced at Crayson, bowed her head slightly and said, "Yes." Then she gazed back out window.

The other man said, "It is a bad thing to be deaf."

"Yes," Crayson said. "I will not bother the fellow anymore."

For the rest of the trip to Savannah, Ellen had to listen to the men talk about "cotton and abolitionists," but Crayson did not speak to her again.

At Savannah, William and Ellen boarded a steamship for Charleston, South Carolina. That night, Ellen dozed in a first-class cabin while William curled up on a pile of cotton bags on the corner of the deck.

The next morning, Ellen was seated at a breakfast table with the captain and several other men, including a slave catcher. Since Ellen's arm was in a sling, William cut up her food.

"You have a very attentive boy," the captain said. "But you had better watch him like a hawk when you get . . . to the North . . . ." The captain warned Ellen that abolitionists were ready to help slaves escape.

The slave catcher rested both elbows on the table and gnawed on a piece of chicken. "I would not take a [slave] to the North under no consideration," he said through a mouthful of half-chewed food.

Dropping the chicken on his plate, the slave catcher leaned back, putting both thumbs in the armholes of his vest. "Now, stranger," he said to Ellen, "if you have made up your mind to sell that there [slave], I am your man. Just [name] your price, and if it isn't out of the way, I will pay for him . . . with hard silver dollars."

Ellen insisted she did not want to sell William. The man continued to pressure her, warning that her boy would run as soon as they reached free soil.

"I think not, sire, I have great confidence in his fidelity," Ellen said.

"Fidevil!" The slave catcher slammed his fist down on the table. His hand hit a coffee cup, spilling hot liquid all over the lap of another passenger.

Ellen stood up. "My rheumatism is bothering me. I shall retire to my cabin."

But Ellen could not hide in her room for the entire trip. Later in the day, she returned to the dining room. William brought her food and drink, and Ellen thanked him. A young officer at the table curled his lip in disapproval.

"I assure you, sir," the officer said. "Nothing spoils a slave . . . as saying thank you. The only way to make a [slave] toe the mark . . . is to storm at him like thunder and keep him trembling like a leaf."

Just then, the officer's slave entered the room and the officer swore viciously at him to demonstrate how a master should act. Ellen forced herself to speak more harshly to William.

She had to play her role to perfection if she wanted to survive.

———◆———

When the steamer reached Charleston, William hailed a carriage and asked the driver to take them to the city's best hotel. Their money was rapidly dwindling, but they had to keep up the appearance of Ellen as a rich gentleman.

They stayed in Planter's Inn. With 10-foot ceilings, silk curtains, polished pine floors, a fireplace, and a four-poster bed in every room, the hotel was luxurious. But neither Ellen nor William could enjoy it. They were still in slave country.

The next morning, Ellen and William went to the customs office on the wharf. Ellen stepped up to the counter. "Two tickets for Philadelphia, please," she said. "One for myself and one for my slave."

The ticket agent studied William. "Do you belong to this gentleman?"

"Yes, sir," William said.

The agent handed Ellen the tickets, "Register your name here, sir, and also the name of your [slave]."

Ellen nodded at her right arm in its sling. "Could you please sign for me?"

The agent frowned. He seemed offended by the request.

"Please, sir, my arm is injured," Ellen said.

The man shoved both hands deep in his pockets. "I shan't do it!" he said loudly.

People were watching. Ellen's mind raced for a solution and sweat dripped nervously between William's shoulder blades. Just then the military officer who had scolded Ellen for being too polite to William came over.

Lubricated by a few too many glasses of brandy, the officer acted like he was Ellen's best friend. "I know his kin like a book," the man insisted.

Since this officer was well known in Charleston, the ticket agent calmed down. Then the captain of the steamship Ellen and William were scheduled to sail on stepped forward.

"I will register the gentleman's name and take the responsibility upon myself." He picked up the pen. "What is your name, sir?" He asked Ellen.

"William Johnson," she replied.

A few minutes later, William and Ellen were on board and headed for Wilmington, North Carolina.

By Christmas Eve, the Crafts had reached Baltimore, Maryland. This slave state bordered free Pennsylvania. Security was strict to guard against fugitives escaping across the border. William settled Ellen in the first-class car and was about to enter the luggage car when a railroad official tapped him on the shoulder.

"Where are you going?"

"To Philadelphia, sir." William explained that his master was in the next carriage.

"Well . . . you had better get him out and be might quick about it because the train will soon be starting," the official said. "It is against my rules to let any man take a slave past here, unless he can satisfy them in the office that he has a right to take him along."

William's heart plummeted. They were so close to freedom. William entered Ellen's car. She was alone and a broad smile lit up her face when she saw her husband. Her smile vanished when William told her what the train official had said.

In the office of the train station, Ellen summoned all her acting skills.

"You wished to see me?" she said to the official.

"It is against our rules, sir," said the man, "to allow any person to take a slave out of Baltimore into Philadelphia, unless he can satisfy us that he has a right to take him along."

"Why is that?" Ellen asked firmly.

The official explained that if a fugitive escaped on the train, the railroad company could be held liable for the cost of the runaway. Therefore, proof of Ellen's ownership was absolutely required.

By this time, a crowd had gathered. Some people clicked their tongues in disapproval. They pitied this poor invalid who did not look anything like an anti-slavery activist. The railroad official shifted from foot to foot. There were rules to follow. He was just doing his job. But the mood of the spectators was making him uncomfortable.

Ellen lifted her chin, willing her voice not to quaver. "I bought tickets in Charleston to pass us through to Philadelphia, and therefore you have no right to detain us here."

But the official refused to back down. "Right or no right, we shan't let you go."

Silence fell over the room. The gathered crowd waited to see who would back down. Ellen and William exchanged a tense glance.

Just then the train whistle blew. The crowd broke apart. Everyone had places to go. The official ran his hands through his hair. "I really don't know what to do."

Ellen just stared at him and waited.

The man finally sighed loudly and threw up his hands. "I calculate it's all right." He claimed he did not want to detain an invalid.

William gave Ellen his arm and she pretended to hobble as quickly as she could to her train car. The train began to pull out of the station. William jumped out of the first-class car, ran alongside the moving train and hauled himself up into the luggage car just as the train picked up speed. He collapsed among the luggage, exhausted. William fell into the sleep of the dead.

Hours later, the train screeched to a halt at the banks of the Susquehanna River. The conductor told the passengers to get off the train and board a ferry. Across the river, another train would take them the final stretch to Philadelphia. Ellen anxiously watched the passengers disembark. William did not appear.

"Have you seen my boy?" she asked the conductor.

He shook his head. "No, sir . . . I have no doubt he is run away and is in Philadelphia, free . . . ."

Panicked, but still trying to maintain her disguise, Ellen hobbled off the train. The night was dark and a cold, steady rain fell. William must have been kidnapped or killed. Should she search for him?

Almost all the passengers were aboard the ferry. In minutes it would depart, leaving her stranded.

Ellen felt her pockets. All she carried were their two train tickets. William had all the money. How could she search for her husband when she did not even have a penny to her name?

Heartbroken, Ellen climbed aboard the ferry.

On the other side of the river, as the train hurtled toward Philadelphia, Ellen still had a part to play. She could not weep or beg for help. She had to remain composed among the other white riders and pretend everything was fine.

While Ellen sat in despair, William snored on. When their train had reached the river crossing, railroad workers decoupled the luggage car, complete with sleeping William, and rolled it onto the ferry. Once on the other shore, the luggage car was linked to the train bound for Philadelphia—the same train on which Ellen was riding.

A few miles out of Philadelphia, a guard entered the luggage car and found William. He shook William's shoulder. "Boy, wake up!" He yelled.

William jolted awake.

"Your master is scared half to death about you."

William's heart froze. Had they been discovered?

"He thinks you have run off," the guard explained.

William sighed with relief. He exited the luggage car and ran into the conductor and some other train workers. They were joking about how frightened William's master had been.

"When you get to Philadelphia," the conductor urged, "run away and leave that cripple. Have your liberty."

William could not even pretend he would ever abandon Ellen. "I shall never run away from such a good master," he said.

The men shrugged, convinced William would feel differently once he reached Philadelphia. They gave him the name of a boarding house run by an abolitionist, in case he changed his mind.

City lights flickered in the distance and the train began to slow. William felt as though "the straps that bound the heavy burden to my back began to pop, and the load to roll off."

Before the train had completely stopped, William jumped off and ran to Ellen's car. It must have taken all their self-restraint not to fall into each other's arms. William retrieved their luggage and hailed a cab. He climbed inside the carriage and sat beside his wife. They were alone.

"Thank God, William," Ellen said. "We are safe." And she took her husband's hand.

The Crafts were not quite safe yet. Philadelphia was a free city in a free state, but slave catchers had the legal right to hunt down fugitives anywhere in the country. Ellen and William stayed with a white Quaker family outside the city for weeks and then made their way to Boston, Massachusetts.

For two years, the dream of freedom in America became a reality for the Crafts. William got a job as a cabinetmaker and Ellen worked as a seamstress. Their marriage was made legal in a church ceremony. The Crafts were active in the anti-slavery movement and told the story of their escape.

Abolitionists convinced Ellen to get a photograph of herself taken dressed as Mr. William Johnson. She did so and the image was printed in anti-slavery literature that spread across the country. Viewers were shocked at a woman who dressed like a man. While Northerners felt admiration at Ellen and William's bravery, Southerners were embarrassed that the Crafts had escaped under their very noses.

But for the Crafts, their terrifying adventure had been worth it for the sake of freedom.

In 1850, Robert Collins hired two slave catchers to catch the Crafts. When the slave catchers arrived in Boston, an army of abolitionists awaited them. They pelted the slave catchers with rotten eggs and sympathetic police arrested them for minor offenses, such as driving their carriage too quickly or lighting cigarettes in public.

According to the 1850 Fugitive Slave Law, all U.S. citizens were legally required to help slave catchers apprehend runaways. When Robert Collins heard how his men were being mistreated, he wrote a protest letter to President Millard Fillmore. The Crafts decided not to wait around. They moved to England on December 11, 1850.

In England, both William and Ellen attended school, quickly learning to read and write. In 1860, William published his memoirs, *Running 1,000 Miles for Freedom*. Although William is the only author listed on the book, scholars are convinced Ellen helped write it.

While living in England, the Crafts had five children. All of them were born into freedom.

INDIAN
OCEAN

MERTZ GLACIER

NINNIS
GLACIER

ANTARCTICA

SOUTH POLE

1. November 10, 1912
Douglas Mawson,
Xavier Mertz, and
Belgrave Ninnis leave
base camp as the
Far Eastern Party.

2. Belgrave falls into
a crevasse and dies.

3. Xavier dies.

4. Douglas escapes
death and returns to
base camp, where he
has to wait almost a
year to go back to
Australia.

1911	1912	1914

Norwegian
explorer Roald
Amundsen is
the first to reach
the South Pole

Douglas Mawson's
expedition sets out
to map Antarctica

World War I
begins

Chapter Two

The Jaws of Terra Incognita

Antarctica cast a spell on Australian geologist
and explorer Douglas Mawson. The continent
was known for mammoth glaciers, a fiery
volcano, and cathedrals of ice. In 1912,
Antarctica lured Douglas into a trap from
which escape would be almost impossible.

The idea of Antarctica had captured the imagination
of explorers for centuries. People of ancient times
imagined a huge landmass lay at the bottom of the
earth that was fertile, rich, and warm. On ancient
maps, this region was labeled *terra incognita* or
"unknown land."

A British sailor made the first documented sighting
of Antarctica in 1820. This led adventurers on an
international race to explore, chart, and claim the
continent.

Douglas Mawson was only 26 years old when he first set foot on Antarctica as part of Ernest Shackleton's 1907 Nimrod expedition. Shackleton was trying to be the first to reach the South Pole. But he was also interested in gathering scientific data, and asked Douglas to come along as the expedition's geologist.

On the Nimrod expedition, Douglas climbed Mount Erebus, at the time the only known active volcano on Antarctica. He was also on the team that reached the magnetic South Pole. In total, Douglas crossed 1,260 miles of frozen terrain.

Douglas claimed that the continent "rivets our souls." As soon as the expedition ended, he began to plan his return to Antarctica.

Terra incognita waited patiently, her icy jaws wide open.

In 1911, Douglas was named commander of the Australian Antarctic Expedition (AAE). Its mission was to map uncharted territory and collect scientific data. The team set sail from Australia aboard the *Aurora* on December 2. A month later, the nose of the *Aurora* butted into the pack ice surrounding Antarctica.

The ship navigated around icebergs and past cliffs of ice before finding harbor in a rocky cove named Commonwealth Bay. The team built its base camp.

While the men planned to remain in Antarctica for only one year, Douglas had brought supplies for two years, just in case winter came early and the *Aurora* was unable to pick them up on time. The scientists unloaded the ship, shared a final supper with the ship's crew, and then the *Aurora* sailed away. It was due to

Aurora

return in one year. Douglas watched his only link with the safe, civilized world sail away into icy seas.

———◆———

In the Southern Hemisphere, it is summer during the month of January. As summer gave way to winter, Antarctica gave the team a taste of her temperament. Mountains funneled 200-mile-per hour winds into frozen valleys and across plains of ice. Wind gusts chiseled ice into sastrugi, which are wave-like ridges on packed snow.

Douglas spent the winter months preparing for the next summer's scientific work. He formed eight, three-man exploration parties. These groups would map the territory and gather data and samples of rocks and minerals, weather patterns, plant and animal life, and glacier formations.

But first, the crew had to endure a winter in Antarctica, surrounded by storms and ice.

Antarctic ice does not stand still. Glaciers creep toward the sea, bending and cracking everything in their path. Ice splits from the pressure to create crevasses. These yawning gaps often hide under the snow, ready to swallow unwary feet.

Although Antarctica is covered in ice, it is a desert. Only eight inches of snow fall each year on the coast and only two inches in the interior. This snow does not melt. Instead, it piles into mountainous drifts waiting to be blown around like colossal blizzards.

Douglas described Antarctica's storms as "grizzly, fierce, and appalling." Blizzards slammed against the wooden hut where the team lived, banging the roof and shaking the walls. When the winds carried the snow out to sea, they left behind an eerie calm. The team members anxiously waited for Antarctica's next mood swing. To pass the time, they prepared for spring.

Douglas would lead the Far Eastern Party. He picked 29-year-old Swiss ski champion Xavier Mertz and 25-year-old soldier Belgrave Ninnis to accompany him. Douglas intended to march 350 miles, deep into the eastern heart of the continent. If all went according to plan, the AAE teams would explore 1,500 miles of Antarctica's unknown coast and interior, more than any previous expedition.

The crew packed the necessary supplies: pickaxes, spades, hammers, surveying equipment, cameras and film, thermometers, binoculars, compasses, harnesses, ropes, fuel, cook stoves.

Each man would receive 32 ounces of food rations each day. This food included pemmican (a paste of dry meat and fat), sugar, butter, powdered milk, biscuits, raisins, chocolate, and tea. Dried seal meat would feed the dog teams. The supplies would be carried on 11-foot sledges pulled by teams of huskies.

The average temperature during an Antarctic summer is -20 degrees Fahrenheit (-29 degrees Celsius). The men sewed extra lining into their tents and packed reindeer-skin sleeping bags. Jackets and pants were made of a windproof material. To guard against frostbite, the men wore two layers of mittens topped by gloves on their hands and reindeer-skin boots on their feet. Heads, ears, and necks were protected by woolen ski masks called helmets, covered by fur-lined hoods.

During the winter, the men made short training excursions. On one of these trips, Douglas and Belgrave cut a cave into the ice about five miles from base camp. They planted a flagpole on a hill above the shelter. The light filtered down into the cave, turning the walls a magical bluish-green.

Belgrave Ninnas christened it Aladdin's Cave.

In mid-October, the penguins returned—a sure sign of the coming summer. Each exploration party made final preparations for breaking camp. On November 3, Douglas called everyone together. Each group's mission was reviewed, and he reminded the men about a critical deadline.

The *Aurora* would return to pick up the team on January 15, 1913. Everyone must be back at base camp before that date.

"At all costs," Douglas warned, "we have to be ready to go home by then!" Ships that waited too late to depart Antarctica risked getting frozen in the ice. If that happened, nobody would go home.

At noon on Sunday, November 10, the Far Eastern Party set off. Seventeen dogs, three sledges, and three men. Only one of them would return.

Xavier Mertz and Belgrave Ninnis with
one of the sledges and dog teams

———◆———

Antarctica made the Far Eastern Party work for every mile. Two massive glaciers took an eternity to cross. Hidden crevasses nearly swallowed the dogs and men. Belgrave Ninnis came down with a case of snow blindness, a condition that felt like someone was rubbing grit across his eyeballs. Some days, storms forced the team to remain in its tent, while on other days, the sun's glare turned the snow to mush and the sledges barely moved.

The group was clocking fewer miles east than Douglas had hoped. He wrote in his diary, "Things are looking serious for our onward progress." He kept his eye on the calendar. They had to turn back early enough to meet the January 15 departure date.

Douglas was pleased with his travel partners. Belgrave, who they nicknamed "Cherub" because of his round, pink cheeks, was eager to learn and easy to like. Xavier Mertz was always cheerful, no matter how bad the weather or how long the march.

The three men developed a routine. Every day, they saved some of their lunch rations for afternoon "tea." Everyone pitched in to set up camp. The men erected the tent together. Then, Douglas cooked supper, Xavier made up their beds, and Belgrave tended to the dogs. After dinner, the men wrote in their diaries or scribbled letters to loved ones. Douglas wrote to his fiancée, "I have two good companions."

Little did any of them know that Antarctica was preparing to snatch one of those "good companions."

As food supplies decreased, fewer sledges were needed. On December 12, the men discarded a sledge with worn-out runners. They also tossed out empty cans, old sacks, and boots and gloves with holes. The lighter the load, the faster the dogs could pull.

Xavier skied at the front of their group. Douglas followed on the lighter sledge, and Belgrave brought up the rear on the sledge that carried the tent and most of the food. This sledge was also pulled by the best dog team. Douglas figured the most important sledge was safest in the back of the party, so Belgrave would get advance warning of any dangerous terrain.

December 14 was perfect traveling weather. The sun warmed the faces of the men and a light wind blew. Xavier skied about 30 yards ahead of the others. Douglas wrote in his diary as he rode on his sledge. Belgrave walked alongside his dog team, whip in hand to guide the animals. The men were upbeat.

In two days, they would head back to base camp.

Xavier stopped suddenly and raised a ski pole in the air to signal he had just skied across a snow bridge. These natural bridges that formed over crevasses were impossible to avoid in Antarctica. Douglas hollered a warning to Belgrave and then steered his sledge across the bridge. He glanced over his shoulder and saw Belgrave crack his whip to guide his dogs.

Douglas's sledge skidded along and he continued to write. A few seconds later, one of his dogs whined. Douglas looked up. Xavier had stopped skiing and was staring back at the trail, his expression creased with worry. Douglas turned. Belgrave had vanished.

Leaping off his sledge, Douglas ran back up the trail. Where moments earlier there had been a snow bridge, there was now a gaping crevasse.

"Get the rope!" Douglas yelled. He shouted into the gorge. "Cherub! Can you hear me?" The only sound that floated up was a dog's whimper.

Xavier tied a rope around Douglas's waist and held on as Douglas leaned over the edge of the abyss, peering through binoculars. The green-and-blue-tinged walls of the crevasse disappeared into a black pit. About 150 feet down, a ragged ledge of snow jutted out from the wall. Two dogs lay side by side. One was struggling to rise, its back clearly broken, and the other was dead. Beside them were the tent and a food sack. Belgrave was nowhere in sight.

Xavier and Douglas called their friend's name until they grew hoarse. Their rope was too short to even reach the ledge.

"We must accept the bitter truth," Douglas said. "Cherub is dead."

The men grieved for Cherub, but knew they had to act quickly. Most of their supplies lay at the bottom of the crevasse. Douglas's sledge carried one week of rations for three men. They had no dog food. The tent, ground cover, poles, spade, pickax, sledge sail, dishes, Xavier's waterproof pants and helmet, and their six best dogs were gone. Base camp was 320 miles west.

"You know what this means, don't you?" Douglas asked.

Xavier nodded. "We must eat the dogs."

Douglas took longitude and latitude readings to chart the precise location—he named Belgrave's final resting place the Black Crevasse.

A full night's march brought Xavier and Douglas back to where they had camped two days earlier. Douglas dug through the discarded items and found torn wolf-skin gloves, worn-out reindeer-hide boots, and a strap of leather. He fed these to the dogs.

Then Xavier and Douglas cobbled together a shelter with old sledge runners tied to snowshoes, draped with a canvas cloth. The peak of the shelter was only four feet high and so narrow only one man could sit up at a time. This would be their tent for the next 300 miles.

The next task was more difficult, but had to be done. Douglas shot George, the weakest dog. He fed half the carcass to the other dogs, which tore into the meat with frantic hunger.

Xavier could barely force himself to swallow meat sliced from George's hind legs. But to Douglas's surprise, although the dog meat was stringy and rather "musty," it was still "quite good." The men needed to develop a taste for dog meat if they wanted to live long enough to escape Antarctica.

The long march began. Up frozen ridges and down hills of ice. The wind in their faces and the snow at their backs. Day after day.

Hunger clawed at the men's stomachs, but worse was their thirst. A fire was needed to melt the deeply frozen snow, but lighting the stove required putting up the tent. The men marched on and tried to ignore their tongues of sand.

Every few days, a dog collapsed and was carried in the sledge. Douglas and Xavier strapped themselves into the harness and pulled beside those animals that were still able to walk. When the men made camp, Douglas shot the collapsed dog, fed half of it to the surviving animals, and cooked the rest.

They saved the dog liver for themselves. It tasted "repellent," but went down easily. Douglas assumed it was full of nutrients.

After a week of marching, both Xavier and Douglas began to experience frightening symptoms. No amount of water could remove the stinging sensations from their noses and throats. Stabbing stomach cramps made the men double over in pain.

On Christmas day, Douglas was packing up the stove. He had removed his woolen helmet.

"Hold still," Xavier said.

He plucked something off Douglas's left ear and held up a piece of ear-shaped skin. Puzzled, Douglas touched his other ear. A large chunk of skin came away in his hand.

The men looked at each other in alarm. Xavier removed his helmet and tufts of beard and skin sloughed off. The skin at Xavier's temples was raw. Cracks around his nose and mouth oozed liquid—they looked like they had been made with a razor blade.

Neither man had removed his clothing in weeks. Now, despite the cold, they had to see what was happening to their bodies. Skin and hair fell like snow onto their boots.

"The diet of dog does not agree with me," Xavier said gloomily.

That diet was about to end. Ginger, the last surviving dog, collapsed on December 28. Douglas laid her on the sledge and stroked her fur. She had given them everything she had, but still they had to take more.

Knowing their survival depended on it, Douglas and Xavier ate the entire dog, even her eyeballs and brain. Although their bellies were full after this, both men felt hollow at the sight of Ginger's empty harness.

The morning of December 31, a different Xavier climbed out of his sleeping bag. The cheerful, positive man was sullen and silent all day. The next morning the new year dawned with snow and heavy winds— the men could march only five miles. That night, Xavier wrote in his diary, "I cannot eat of dogs any longer. Yesterday the flesh made me feel very sick." Those were the last words he would ever write.

Xavier stayed in his sleeping bag for three days, refusing to eat. Even a biscuit with a pat of butter did not tempt him. While a blizzard raged outside, anxiety flooded Douglas. He must build up Xavier's strength so they could march.

Finally, Douglas convinced Xavier to swallow a little liver.

The sun came out on January 3, but after slipping and stumbling for four miles, Xavier could go no further. Douglas wrote in his diary, "Xavier in a very bad state. Everything depends now on Providence."

Then Douglas began to feel sick, too. He was hit with stomach cramps, dizziness, and nausea, but forced himself to prepare to march. Xavier refused.

"It is suicide to march in bad weather," he said.

"It's suicide to sit here and starve to death," Douglas shot back.

"Tomorrow," Xavier promised. "If the weather is good, I will march tomorrow."

The following day, Xavier made it two miles before collapsing. "My mind goes forward," he said, "but my legs stay here."

Douglas was desperate. He lifted Xavier into the sledge and strapped himself into the harness. The straps dug into his shoulders and his feet slid on the ice. "I will do as well as Ginger . . . ," Douglas told himself and got down on his hands and knees.

He crawled with the sledge for two miles before Xavier's cries stopped him. White frost spotted Xavier's face. He was freezing to death.

Douglas made camp and helped Xavier into his sleeping bag. Then he climbed into his own. Outside the tent, wind howled and the ice groaned.

The men were trapped in a frozen prison 100 miles from base camp.

That night, a stench awoke Douglas. Xavier had soiled himself. As Douglas cleaned him, the man began to rage. In his hallucinations, Xavier thought Douglas was preparing to slaughter him.

"Am I a man or a dog?" His sunken eyes glared at Douglas. "You think I have no courage because I cannot walk, but I show you."

Xavier raised his left hand, its little finger yellow with frostbite. He shoved the finger into his mouth and bit down. Douglas watched in horror as Xavier chomped through bone and cartilage, biting off his finger at the middle joint. Then Xavier spit his finger into the snow. Douglas soothed his friend, bandaged his finger, and tucked him into his sleeping bag.

Morning came. The sun rose. It was a perfect day for marching, but Xavier would never march again. Douglas wrote in his diary, "God help us."

After another night of thrashing and delusions, Xavier finally quieted down and Douglas fell asleep. A couple hours later, he jerked awake. The only sound was the unending flap of the tent in the wind. He reached out his arm and touched Xavier's face. His friend was cold and stiff.

Antarctica had claimed another member of the Far Eastern Party.

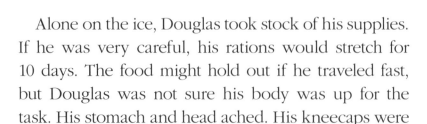

Alone on the ice, Douglas took stock of his supplies. If he was very careful, his rations would stretch for 10 days. The food might hold out if he traveled fast, but Douglas was not sure his body was up for the task. His stomach and head ached. His kneecaps were knobs of skinless flesh. Boils festered on his waist and shoulders.

Exhaustion overwhelmed Douglas and he longed to lie down forever.

From the depths of Douglas's brain came the voice of one of his favorite poets, Robert Service. *Buck up! Do your damndest and fight! It's the plugging away that will win you the day.* These words pushed Douglas to his feet.

Xavier's waterproof coat and an old food bag became a sail. Douglas cut the sledge in half and used pieces of it to build a mast. He would let the wind pull him forward whenever possible to conserve his energy. Douglas cooked the last of the dog meat, including Ginger's liver. Then there was only one task left.

As the wind rose and the sky darkened, Douglas built a cairn of snow around Xavier's body. He read the burial service once again, as he had done for Belgrave. Then he took two halves of a sledge runner and thrust these into the cairn in the shape of a cross.

Only a mile into the march, Douglas felt a strange squelching pain in his feet. He sat down and removed a boot. As he pulled off his socks, the sole of his foot slid off with it. The bottom of his foot was a mass of watery tissue. Douglas's heart sank. He could not march 100 miles on rotten feet.

Douglas smeared lanolin oil on both feet. Then he carefully removed the skin from inside his dirty socks and lashed it to the bottom of his feet with bandages. Six pairs of socks went on next. It was all he could do.

Mile after excruciating mile, Douglas marched, his feet worsening by the day. One night, as Douglas lay in his sleeping bag, he realized it was January 15, 1913. The *Aurora* waited at base camp to take them home. Winter was just around the corner, and the captain would not stall the departure for long. Douglas tried to march faster.

On January 17, he was crossing a snowy spine at the top of a glacier, the sledge attached to his waist by a rope. The snow under Douglas's feet was smooth and the sledge slid easily. Suddenly, he sank up to his thighs. Douglas studied the snow closely. He made out the thin line of a crevasse heading south. So Douglas turned north, where the snow looked solid.

Seconds later, he plummeted into nothingness.

The rope around Douglas's waist jerked, halting his free fall. As he spun slowly in circles, a quick glance over one shoulder revealed that he was dangling above a black chasm. One of Antarctica's endless gorges had him in its jaws.

Douglas felt the sledge creep toward the edge of the crevasse and he slipped a little lower into the pit. "So this is the end," he thought.

Suddenly the sledge stopped. It had butted up against a ridge of snow. The crevasse walls were as smooth as glass, impossible to grip. Douglas's only life-line was the rope around his waist. The rope was knotted every 12 inches. He needed to climb up, one knot at a time.

Douglas doubted he had the strength. Closing his eyes, Douglas stretch out one thin arm and grasped the first knot.

His palm screamed as the rope cut into his rotting skin. Douglas ignored the pain and lunged forward with his other arm. Hand over hand, he climbed 14 feet until he was finally level with the edge of the crevasse. Bracing his arms on the snow, Douglas tried to heave himself up.

Suddenly, the snow under his arms broke away and he plummeted all the way back down. Chest heaving and limbs trembling, Douglas hung limply over the abyss.

On the back of his belt was a knife. One quick slice on the rope and his suffering would end.

But on the heels of this despair, faces appeared in Douglas's mind: his beloved fiancée, Belgrave and Xavier, the AAE team. The poem echoed in Douglas's head again. *Buck up! Try again!*

Slowly, painfully, Douglas hauled himself back up the rope. This time, he thrust his legs out of the crevasse first and launched onto solid ground. Then, Douglas passed out.

He woke an hour later and tried to march but found himself nearly paralyzed by fear. A crevasse could lie under every step.

Each day was harder than the one before. The winds grew stronger, the slopes steeper, and Douglas weaker. His hair fell out by the handful and his nails fell off. His teeth rattled in their sockets and his jaws ached. All he had left to eat was pemmican and scorched dog liver. But he trudged on.

The afternoon of January 28, Douglas noticed a dark blur in the landscape ahead. Unaware of any rock formations in this region, he plodded forward to investigate. Instead of a rock, Douglas found "miraculous, marvelous good fortune."

The team had been searching for him. A freshly built cairn was draped with black cloth. He tore it open and pulled out a waterproof bag. Inside, he found food and a note.

Aladdin's Cave is only 21 miles from here.

The Aurora *waits in the bay.*

All other exploration parties have returned to base camp.

The time and date were recorded at the bottom of the note. He had missed the search party by just six hours! Douglas's crushing disappointment at having missed the search party eased a little when he saw what the men had left for him.

The food bag brimmed with tins of pemmican, sugar, butter, chocolate, and oranges. Douglas hoisted the sail, hopped on board, and let the sledge ride the wind while he gorged on biscuits and chocolate.

On February 1, Douglas finally caught site of the flagpole on Aladdin's Cave. On bloody feet and trembling legs, he stumbled forward. That night, Douglas slept inside walls for the first time in months. The next day he would reach base camp!

But Antarctica was not ready to release Douglas from her icy grip. The next morning, a powerful blizzard struck. Gloom blanketed Douglas's mind, and although he was only five miles from camp, he wanted to surrender. How could he walk on crippled feet? Why did he still feel so sick when he was eating proper rations? His iron will was slipping away.

Five days later, the storm finally stopped. Douglas emerged from the cave, dragging his sledge behind him. Head down and goggles on, he bent into the wind and marched. Several hours later, he stopped and removed his goggles. Commonwealth Bay lay before him.

With a mixture of hope and dread, Douglas studied the harbor. The *Aurora* was not at anchor. His gaze landed on a dark speck at the mouth of the bay where a plume of black smoke rose into the sky. The ship was leaving. Douglas was marooned in Antarctica.

To his own surprise, Douglas felt nothing. "What does it matter," he told himself. "This terrible chapter of my life is coming to a close." He resumed marching.

A half mile farther, Douglas stepped over a rise in the ground and the hut came into view. No smoke rose from the stovepipe on the roof and the camp appeared deserted. Then a movement by the harbor caught Douglas's eye. Three figures bent over something on the ground.

Douglas raised one weak arm and waved. He tried to call out, but could only rasp. One of the figures stood up and looked in his direction. Suddenly, all three men began to shout and ran toward him. Douglas collapsed.

Douglas Mawson
recuperating at base camp

An eternity passed before Frank Bickerton, one of team's engineers, bent over the fallen man. Bickerton lifted the living skeleton and propped him on the sledge, searching the frostbitten face. He was no one Bickerton recognized.

"My God!" he cried. "Which one are you?"

Soon, five men surrounded Douglas, hammering him with questions. As if in a dream, he told what had happened to Belgrave and Xavier. Tears ran down the men's faces and Douglas's own throat grew tight with emotion. But something else worried him, too.

"The ship? Where is the ship?"

He saw the answer in their expression. The *Aurora* had left. These men had stayed behind to search for the Far Eastern Party.

Douglas had survived, but it would be another 10 months before he escaped Antarctica.

Douglas Mawson recuperated at base camp while he waited for the *Aurora* to return. Despite rest and good food, he suffered from swollen legs, sharp headaches, and intense anxiety. The team doctor was mystified about the cause of these ailments.

In February 1914, Douglas returned to Australia and was hailed as a national hero. He married his fiancée. Despite his grueling experience on the AAE, Douglas succumbed to Antarctica's charms one more time. In 1930, he led the British, Australian, and New Zealand Antarctic Research Expedition. However, on this voyage, Douglas explored terra incognita by ship and plane rather than on foot.

Not until the 1970s did scientists finally determine what killed Xavier Mertz and sickened Douglas Mawson. They were poisoned by a toxic dose of vitamin A from eating dog liver. Just three ounces of liver from a sled dog is enough to kill an adult human.

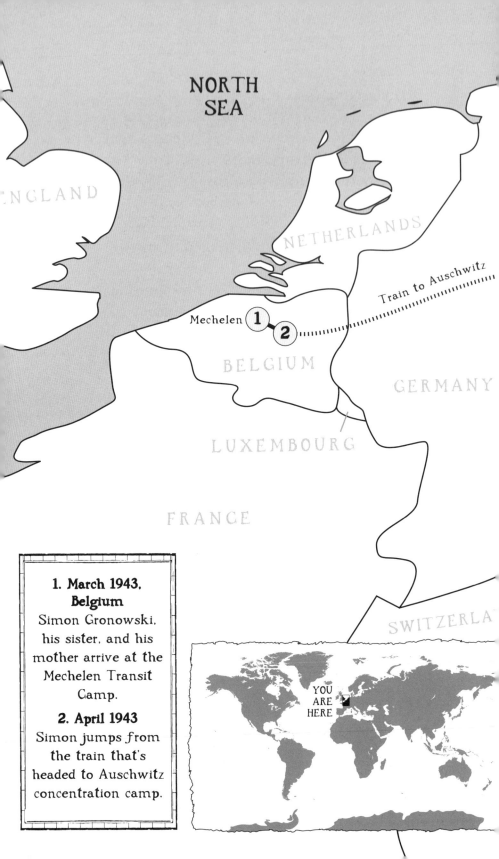

NORTH
SEA

ENGLAND

NETHERLANDS

Train to Auschwitz

Mechelen ① ②

BELGIUM

GERMANY

LUXEMBOURG

FRANCE

SWITZERLA

**1. March 1943,
Belgium**
Simon Gronowski,
his sister, and his
mother arrive at the
Mechelen Transit
Camp.

2. April 1943
Simon jumps from
the train that's
headed to Auschwitz
concentration camp.

YOU
ARE
HERE

1940	1943	1945

Germany invades
Belgium
    Simon escapes
    from the train
    World War II
    ends

Chapter Three

Death Train

On April 19, 1943, German soldiers herded hundreds of Jewish men, women, and children out of the Mechelen Transit Camp near Brussels, Belgium, and into the cars of a waiting train. Simon Gronowski, 11 years old, held tightly to his mother's hand.

German authorities told the Jews they were being sent to a labor camp in Eastern Europe. Once there, officials promised, they would be well-fed and allowed to live comfortably.

There was nothing to fear, they were told.

But Simon was very afraid. When the heavy metal door of the train slid shut, only one thing was on his mind—escape.

Simon Gronowski's life had been carefree before Germany invaded Belgium in 1940. He lived with his parents, Leon and Chana, and his older sister, Ita, in a suburb of Brussels. The Gronowskis owned a leather goods shop and the apartment above it, where the family lived. In the summers, they vacationed for a month by the sea. In the winter, they went to the movies and dined out on Russian eggs with French fries. "I had a radiant childhood," Simon recalled.

Simon had a talent for getting into trouble. Too often, he settled arguments with his fists. Fascinated by fire, he almost burned their building down more than once. Simon's recklessness drove his parents crazy.

One day, this recklessness would serve him well.

Adolf Hitler, leader of the ruthless Nazi Party, became chancellor of Germany in 1933. Hitler expanded Germany's military forces and invaded neighboring countries. On September 1, 1939, Germany went too far when it attacked Poland. In response, Great Britain and France declared war on Germany, and World War II began.

Hitler seemed unstoppable. By the spring of 1940, Germany occupied Poland, Denmark, Norway, Belgium, the Netherlands, and France. In addition to dominating Europe, Hitler had another goal—to rid the continent of all Jews.

Nazi policies evolved during the war to improve the chances of achieving this goal. When World War II ended in 1945, the Nazis had murdered 6 million Jews and millions of other people whose only crime was being different from what the Nazis claimed was the ideal human.

Simon's carefree life changed on May 10, 1940. That morning, the sky over Brussels turned black with German bombers. As the German army sliced through Belgian defenses, the Gronowskis left their home and headed west toward the French border with thousands of other Belgians. All were attempting to escape the brutal treatment they were sure would follow the German invasion. But soon, the German tanks and planes veered westward, too.

Bombs began to rain down in the night. Leon and Chana grabbed their children and sought shelter in a forest. When Simon emerged from the woods the next morning, ruined houses still smoldered and dead bodies lined the roadside.

The German army had reached France, so no sanctuary would be found there. The Gronowskis headed home. On June 5, 1940, they arrived back in Brussels to learn their nation had surrendered. Nazi officials and German military officers moved in and took over.

German authorities ordered all Jews to register with the government. Food was rationed during the war. If a person did not register, he did not receive an identity card. Without an identify card, he could not get food rations for items such as meat, butter, and sugar. So, Leon Gronowski registered his family.

The word "JEW" was stamped in big, red letters across the fronts of their identity cards.

A few months later, German authorities took control of Jewish companies. Leon had to register his store with the government and hang a sign in the window that said "Jewish business."

Slowly, the Nazis tightened their noose. Jews were no longer allowed to have radios or go to public swimming pools or the movie theater. Simon's sister, Ita, was banned from attending high school with non-Jews. In June 1942, the Nazis ordered Jews to wear yellow stars on their jackets. Simon was exempt because he was too young, but Ita had to wear one. She hated being "stared at like a rare animal."

Few dared disobey the rule. If a Jew was caught in public without the star, he would be taken to the headquarters of the secret police, the Gestapo. There were horror stories of what was done in the basement of that building.

The man responsible for carrying out Hitler's Jewish policy in Belgium was Kurt Asche. In his early 30s, Asche wore thick glasses and his face was bloated from too many nights of heavy drinking. Asche had the power of life and death over Belgium's Jews, and he seemed to enjoy that power.

Two types of Jewish leaders emerged in Belgium—people who tried to cooperate with the Nazis and people who tried to destroy the Nazis. In the fall of 1941, Nazi officials organized the Jewish Council of Belgium, called the AJB. This group of wealthy, educated Jewish men met weekly with Asche at his office. He notified the council of new rules, and the AJB was responsible for passing this information on to Jews across the country. These Jewish elders believed cooperation with the Nazis was the key to survival.

Another group of Jewish leaders believed just the opposite. They were the partisans. These men and women were resistance fighters. They met in secret and worked to sabotage German war efforts and assassinate Nazi leaders.

Simon Gronowski knew nothing about the AJB or the partisans. He was just a boy who wanted to have fun. And he did, even as the war raged around him.

Simon's Boy Scout troop met every Saturday. They held races, played games, and practiced the Boy Scout moral code—*do at least one good deed every day.* At Boy Scout camp, Simon learned to navigate by the stars. He also practiced Morse code and knot tying.

While other Jews went into hiding or fled Europe, Leon and Chana Gronowski tried to live as normally as possible. They were confident that things could not get worse.

Unfortunately, they were wrong.

On January 15, 1941, high-ranking Nazi officials met in Wannsee, Germany, to work out the details of what they called the "Final Solution to the Jewish Question." The previous year, Hitler had decided to eliminate all the Jews of Europe. He wanted to kill 11 million people.

The men at Wannsee did not discuss whether this policy was right or wrong. They had gathered to figure out how to implement the plan. Their solution was genocide, what we today call the Holocaust.

During the 1930s, the Germans had built concentration camps. These were used to hold political prisoners and other people the Nazis labeled as "undesirables," such as homosexuals and the Romani.

Once World War II began, these labor camps housed thousands of Jews and prisoners of war, who were often worked to death.

However, the mission of the Final Solution was to kill millions of Jews quickly. The Nazis built death camps to achieve their goal. The first was called Chelmo, which opened in December 1941. At Chelmo, Jews were gassed to death in vans, a messy, time-consuming process.

Selection at Auschwitz, summer 1944
photo credit: Yad Vashem

Other death camps followed, with the largest at Auschwitz. With practice and inventiveness, the Germans became more efficient murderers. Auschwitz was equipped with four gas chambers, where Zyklon B poison gas was administered to prisoners in shower-like facilities.

Throughout the territory under German control, Jews were rounded up and sent to transit camps, where they were held for a few weeks or months until there were enough people to fill a train. Then, Nazi officials told the Jews they were being sent to a labor camp. The Jews were herded into cattle cars, shipped off like livestock, and slaughtered. At the height of its operation, more than 6,000 people a day were killed at Auschwitz.

———◆———

In the spring of 1942, Kurt Asche was told it was time to begin deporting the Jews from Belgium to Auschwitz. Asche ordered the AJB to report to Gestapo headquarters.

"Jews are needed for service outside of Belgium," he lied. "You are responsible for compiling the list of workers to be deported."

Only non-Belgian Jews were to be sent in the first batch of 10,000 people. These should be both males and females between the ages of 16 and 50.

"At least 10 percent of the people you choose should be elderly and ill," Asche added.

The council members were immediately suspicious. Why were the old and the sick being sent to a work camp? "Where are you sending these people?" one council member dared ask.

"East," was all Asche would say. If the AJB did not compile a list, Asche would order soldiers to grab Jews off the street.

The council did as it was told. By the end of July, the Nazis had a list of 56,000 Jews to deport. From this list, the AJB had to select 1,500 people to be on the first train. Letters arrived in the mailboxes of these unlucky Jews. They were ordered to report to the Mechelen Transit Camp. If they refused, they would be arrested.

A list of supplies was provided: nonperishable food for 14 days, work boots, two blankets, and a sweater. This list was all part of the lie.

On July 27, the first Jews arrived at Mechelen, but only about half of those ordered to actually showed up. Asche was furious. He needed to fill the train, so he ordered the SS, the elite German police force, to round up Jews.

Military trucks circled Jewish neighborhoods. SS officers searched the houses one by one. People were rousted from bed and given only minutes to pack before being herded into the backs of trucks. Shouts of "Faster, keep walking!" cut through the night. Non-Jewish neighbors peeked through their curtains, but no one dared intervene.

The next morning, the atmosphere in these neighborhoods was leaden. No children played in the street. No women walked to the grocery store. The people fortunate enough not to have been taken remained indoors.

Many Jews did resist what was happing. In 1942, partisans formed the Jewish Defense Committee. Members of this group raided military depots and police stations to steal guns and ammunition. They assassinated Belgian collaborators, people who helped the Germans. The Defense Committee hid thousands of Jewish children with non-Jewish families and forged false identity papers for Jews in hiding.

Partisans also printed and distributed underground newspapers to spread the truth about the progress of the war. In these newspapers, partisans urged all Jews to go into hiding before it was too late.

In the summer of 1942, Leon and Chana Gronowski finally decided it was too dangerous to continue to live in their home. Ita had received an order to report to Mechelen for deportation. When authorities realized she was a Belgian citizen, they sent her home. Only non-Belgian Jews were being deported at this time. The family had dodged a bullet, but for how long?

Leon put his business equipment into storage, along with the family's possessions. They rented their apartment out to the parents of one of Simon's friends from Boy Scouts, the Rouffaerts, and the Gronowskis moved to a neighborhood on the edge of Brussels. Chana removed the yellow stars from their coats and hid their identity cards. The family would live under the radar. Without identity cards, they could not get food rations. But everyone tightened their belts and Leon sold some of their stored belongings to get cash.

However, the Gronowskis did not fully grasp the danger they faced. When they moved, they took the family dog. Every evening, Leon and Chana took the animal for a walk. Ita still went out with her friends and Simon still ran about the neighborhood with his Scout buddies. The family was too visible.

The morning of March 17, 1943, Simon and his mother and sister were eating breakfast. The doorbell rang and they all jumped. The buzz was loud and demanding.

The Gronowskis had planned for this moment. If the police came to their door, they would escape through the garden. The doorbell rang again. Simon looked at his mother for guidance. But she seemed paralyzed.

Moments later, two men appeared in the kitchen doorway. "Gestapo!" one barked. "IDs."

Simon's mother handed over their identity cards. One man scanned the cards. "Where is Leon Gronowski?"

"My husband died," Chana lied. Leon was actually in the hospital being treated for an infection.

The Gestapo herded the Gronowskis out. The dog was tied to the banister. Simon hoped one of his neighbors would hear the pup bark and untie him. Simon knew he would not be home any time soon.

The Gronowskis were taken to Gestapo headquarters and locked into a basement room with other arrested Jews. The names of previous prisoners were scribbled over the room's tired white walls. Light peeked through barred windows. Simon watched the feet of passersby and longed to be one of them.

Mechelen Transit Camp

Hour after hour, the family waited on a hard, wooden bench. Simon's stomach growled and he was incredibly thirsty, but they were not given food or drink. Occasionally, the door opened and new prisoners were shoved in. Before long, 50 people were crammed into the room. No one spoke, but noise soaked through the walls from other rooms. The meaty smack of fists on flesh. The cries of people being tortured. The staccato bark of Gestapo agents.

The next afternoon, everyone was loaded into tarp-covered trucks. As the vehicle drove through the city, Simon peeked through a gap in the tarp. The sun was shining and the sky was a beautiful robin's-egg blue. But the sunshine refused to squeeze under the tarp. The faces of the people around Simon looked grayish-green in the dim light.

When the truck stopped and everyone was ordered out, Simon found himself in a huge courtyard surrounded by army barracks. This was the Mechelen Transit Camp. The Jews would stay here until they were deported.

Simon followed his mother and sister into a room with several long tables manned by SS officers. The Jews had to turn over all their money, wristwatches, and jewelry. Then each was given a cardboard sign with a registration number written on it. These signs had to be worn around their necks. Simon was number 1234. He would be the 1,234th person transported on the next train headed for Auschwitz.

Mechelen barracks had two dormitory wings. Simon and his mother were housed together, but Ita was sent to a different dorm. Each room housed 100 inmates in wooden bunk beds. Straw mattresses were drenched in sweat and urine and crawled with lice.

Every day in Mechelen followed a routine. A guard yelled, "Jews, get up!" at 6 a.m. Simon and his mother raced down the stairs to the bathrooms. There were only 10 toilets for 1,500 people.

Simon did not look forward to meal time. Bread, thin cabbage soup, and a teaspoon of sugar and jam was breakfast, lunch, and dinner. The only reason the Gronowskis did not starve to death was because the deportees were allowed to receive packages from friends and relatives. When Simon's father was released from the hospital and discovered his family had been taken, he went into hiding and secretly contacted the Rouffaerts. They sold the items the Gronowskis had put into storage and used the proceeds to send care packages to Simon's mother.

As one day dragged into another, Simon made friends. He missed his father, but he had enough to eat and was with his mother and sister. The guards were mean, but their anger was never targeted at him.

Other deportees were not so fortunate. One night, everyone was roused from bed and ordered into the courtyard. A guard led a young man in handcuffs to the center of the yard.

The man's face was swollen and bruised.

An SS officer screamed at the people lined up. "You should be pleased! The runaway has been caught."

Simon shivered in the cool night air. The officer ranted about how everyone would have been punished if this runaway had not been caught. "Spit on the mangy dog!" he ordered.

No one moved.

The officer called for a volunteer to whip the prisoner. Still no one moved.

The officer beat the man himself. The prisoner died later that night.

As March became April, the number of Jews in the camp swelled. Toilets overflowed. Rations got skimpier. Lice jumped from person to person. Everyone expected to be deported any day.

Partisans outside of camp plotted ways to sabotage the deportation machine. Youra Livchitz was a Russian-born Jewish doctor with friends in the Jewish Defense Committee. He tried to convince them to ambush the next deportation train and free the Jews inside. Everyone refused.

The job was too dangerous.

Livchitz turned to two of his childhood friends for help. Robert Maistriau and Jean Frankelman had been in Boy Scouts with Livchitz. Just like Simon, they had been taught the Scout moral code: *Do at least one good deed every day.* The trio vowed to ambush the next train themselves.

A network of resisters inside camp was also busy. Albert Clement was a Jewish prisoner assigned to the camp maintenance department. When special supplies were needed, a guard accompanied Clement to a local hardware store. The shopkeeper was a partisan, and he slipped things into a box when the guard was not looking—saws, screwdrivers, hammers, and money. Clement passed these items to partisans in camp.

Information was smuggled in as well. One inmate received a bag of macaroni from a friend outside of camp. The friend had scribbled a message on tiny scraps of paper and shoved these inside the noodles. The message said that a rescue attempt was being planned. Everyone should be prepared to escape from the train if they got the chance.

Simon vowed to be ready in case he had to jump from the train. He practiced leaping off his top bunk over and over. When the Gronowskis lived in Brussels, Simon often jumped off the city tram while it was in motion. "I was a specialist," he said later.

As Simon perfected his jumping skills, Youra Livichitz and his friends prepared their ambush.

They purchased a lantern and covered it with red paper. In the dark, the lantern looked like a signal light. They planned to put it on the tracks to stop the train. Then, the three men would use wire cutters to open the train car and release the deportees. From that point on, everyone would have to fend for himself.

Suddenly, the time for preparation was over. On April 15, 1943, Kurt Asche informed the Jewish Council the deportation train would leave in four days.

On her last night in Mechelen, Chana Gronowski wrote a letter to her husband. "Goodbye until the lovely bright day when the sun rises for us . . . and I am with you and our children again . . . ." These were her last words to her husband.

Simon hugged Ita goodbye. She was not scheduled for deportation yet. That night, Chana gave Simon a 50-franc note she had received from a partisan. "Put it in your sock," she said.

On April 19, the people scheduled for deportation waited anxiously to be called to the courtyard. As number 1,234, Simon had a long wait. In the afternoon, numbers 1,200 to 1,250 were ordered to report to the train. Simon followed his mother into the courtyard. Ita stood in the barracks window waving goodbye.

The train car door stood four feet off the ground, so guards had placed a stepladder in front of it. Simon climbed inside the cattle car. Straw covered the floor and the air was thick with the scent of previous riders—both animal and human. A bucket to use as a toilet stood in one corner.

Simon squeezed between the dozens of other people crammed inside. The guard slid the heavy door closed and the lock clicked. A slim ray of light shone through the barred hatch in the roof. The people were silent except for the rasps of their terrified breathing.

Hours passed as the other cars were loaded. Simon's mother found space in the corner of the car and sat down, pulling her son down beside her. She put her arms around her son, and Simon leaned his head on her shoulder. The air was thick and hot. When the train finally began to move, the rhythm of its wheels lulled Simon. His eyelids grew heavy.

The cobblestone road out of Brussels was wet from the rain that had fallen earlier that day. Livchitz, Maistriau, and Frankelman pedaled in silence. The sky was overcast, but when the clouds parted, a full moon made it almost as light as day.

The spot chosen for the ambush was between the towns of Boortmeebeck and Haacht. A bend in the train track and the thick cover of woods made the location perfect. The men hid their bikes in the brush alongside the road. Robert Maistriau set the red lantern on the track, and the men took their positions.

The men's nerves were stretched tight. They started at the sound of the wind in the trees and the distant lowing of cattle. Livchitz carried a pistol, although he had never fired one in his life. Maistriau said he felt an adventurous thrill, but "I knew this wasn't a game, [it was] . . . life and death."

The ambushers did not know it, but some deportees had already escaped the train. The Belgian train engineer knew what cargo he carried, and he deliberately slowed to a walking pace when he crossed intersections or turned corners. People inside some cars had managed to break through their roof hatches and climb on top of the train. When it slowed, they jumped.

Simon awoke to a cool breeze blowing on his face. While he had dozed, a group had managed to break open the door and now it stood wide open. Simon's mother took his hand and led him forward. He believed his mother was "leading me to freedom and life."

A line of people had formed by the door, and one by one, they jumped. Suddenly, it was Simon's turn. He lay down on his belly and dangled his feet over the side. His legs were too short to reach the foothold. Chana Gronowski held her son by his shoulders, slowly lowering him until his feet landed on the step.

The engine roared and trees were a dark blur alongside the track. Simon looked up. His mother leaned toward him, hair whipping over her face. "Train is going too fast," she yelled. These were the last words Simon ever heard from his mother.

"I'm jumping now!" he yelled. The moment he practiced for had arrived. Simon jumped.

The train rounded the bend, thundering toward the red lantern. The engineer pulled the brakes and they screeched in protest. As the train ground to a halt, Livchitz fired his gun twice at the front car, which held German soldiers. Robert Maistriau and Jean Frankelman dashed forward, wire cutters in hand.

Maistriau wrestled with barbed wire lashed across one door. The clouds parted and the moon spotlighted him. Finally, the wire fell away and Maistriau yanked the door open.

"Get out!" he cried. "Hurry!"

The people inside began to push and shove. Some were trying to get out, but others were holding them back. "It's forbidden," they warned, fearing the anger of the guards. Those who did manage to get out ran into the nearby woods.

The guards had remained inside the front car when the two gunshots rang out, afraid an army of partisans was attacking them. But when no more shots were fired, guards spilled out of the train. Some entered the woods to pursue Livchitz, while others headed down the tracks to check on the deportees.

Youra Livchitz, Robert Maistriau, and Jean Frankelman all fled into the woods. After a brief chase, the guards gave up and boarded the train. The journey east resumed.

———◆———

When Simon jumped, he landed like a cat. He stood up and watched the train move away. The great, black monster still held his mother. Surely, she would soon jump, too.

Then, the train screeched to a halt. Simon decided to fetch his mother and began to run toward the train. Suddenly, shots rang out. Simon halted. A moment later, guards appeared and some headed in his direction. Simon turned and ran down a hill and into the woods.

He walked all night. To forget about his mother and the soldiers and the guns, Simon thought about his dog. He sang scouting songs and whistled songs from his sister's favorite record. For hours, he climbed hills, crossed fields, and waded through mud.

At dawn, Simon found himself in a little village. He knocked on the door of the first house he came to. A woman answered. Her eyebrows rose at the sight of the thin, filthy child before her.

"I was playing with my friends in the next village and I got lost," Simon said.

The woman went to fetch her husband. He was the town's police officer. The man listened to Simon's lie and then left the house. Simon waited, his stomach churning in fear.

When the police officer returned, he said, "I know everything. You were on the Jewish train."

Simon swallowed, too terrified to speak. Was the Gestapo already on the way? But the officer continued. "We are good Belgians. You don't have to fear us."

With that, Simon's story poured out. When Simon explained his mother was still on the train, the policeman held him as he wept.

The couple fed Simon and cleaned and repaired his clothes. That afternoon, one of their friends drove Simon to a nearby town. It was for a moment such as this that his mother had given him the 50-franc note. He pulled the money from his sock and bought a train ticket to Brussels. When he reached the city, Simon took the tram to his old house. Mrs. Rouffaert answered the door. She gasped when she saw him. "How is it that you are here?"

"I jumped off the train," Simon said.

Months of hiding followed. During that time, Simon thought about the moment he had jumped from the train. He believed he had been guided "by my mother, by my spirit of revolt and my desire for freedom."

In total, 231 deportees escaped from Simon's train. Of these, 23 people died from falls or were shot by German guards. Youra Livchitz, Robert Maistriau, and Jean Frankelman all continued working against the Germans. Livchitz was betrayed by a double agent and executed in 1944. Frankelman and Maistriau were arrested and sent to concentration camps. They both survived the war.

Simon's family was not so fortunate. His sister, Ita, was deported to Auschwitz in September 1943 and gassed upon arrival. Simon never discovered why his mother did not jump from the train that fateful night. No record was ever found of Chana Gronowski, so it is assumed she died at Auschwitz. Simon spent 17 months in hiding until Belgium was liberated in September 1944. Leon Gronowski was reunited with his son after the war ended, but died two months later.

Simon Gronowski became a lawyer when he grew up so he could fight for justice.

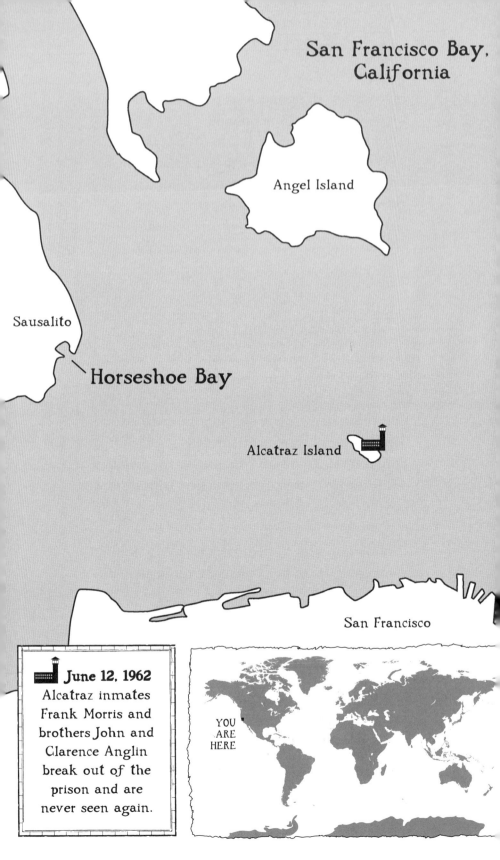

San Francisco Bay,
California

Angel Island

Sausalito

Horseshoe Bay

Alcatraz Island

San Francisco

June 12, 1962
Alcatraz inmates
Frank Morris and
brothers John and
Clarence Anglin
break out of the
prison and are
never seen again.

YOU
ARE
HERE

1934   1962   1963

Alcatraz opens   Three inmates   Alcatraz is
as a federal   escape   closed
penitentiary

Chapter Four

Breaking the Rock

Alcatraz federal penitentiary was escape-proof.
Nicknamed "The Rock," the prison loomed
like a battleship in the middle of San Francisco
Bay. Bone-chilling water surrounded the island,
and powerful tides waited to drag a swimmer
out of the bay into the vast Pacific Ocean.

During its three decades as a prison, inmates tried to escape Alcatraz, but they always failed. Capture or death awaited any man who tried to break out of the Rock. The prison's reputation as escape-proof was solid.

Until the morning of June 12, 1962. Three inmates disappeared from their cells and were never seen again. When their ingenious escape was discovered, the Rock's reputation was shattered.

◆

One misty morning in April 1954, a prison boat slid alongside the dock on Alcatraz Island. From the balcony of the staff apartment building, the guards' wives watched new inmates disembark. A short, wiry man hobbled down the gangplank, his legs and wrists chained.

Alan West was a veteran of prison life. This car thief had served nine years in prison by his 25th birthday, and had made several escape attempts. The prison officials who transferred him to Alcatraz were convinced he would never find a way off the Rock. But from the moment Alan West set foot on the island, he was looking for a way out.

Alcatraz Island
photo credit: Christian Mehlführer

As a bus drove the new inmates from the dock to the cell house, Alan studied the layout of the prison grounds. Four guard towers eyed inmates from all directions. In front of the three-story cell house was a recreation yard surrounded by a cement wall topped by barbed wire. North of the rec yard was the industry building, where inmates manufactured gloves, clothing, and brushes.

At the cell house, Alan's chains and cuffs were removed and he was issued a uniform. A long corridor called Broadway cut the cell house in half. Three tiers of cells lined each side. These were cell block B and cell block C. At each end of Broadway, a gun gallery ran the width of the building. Armed guards stationed in these ceiling-level observation decks overlooked the entire cell house.

Initially a military fort, Alcatraz could house 500 inmates. However, it never held more than 260 people. Cell block A, located on the far side of B block, was empty. D block, better known as "seg," for segregation, was reserved for troublemakers.

An officer locked Alan in his cell and tossed him a rule book. The cell was stark. A cot, sink with one faucet, toilet, and a desk riveted to the wall made up his new home. If Alan stood in the middle of the room and held his arms out, his fingers could touch both walls.

Alan hated Alcatraz. Bells or whistles signaled inmates to stand for a cell count, go to meals, report for work, or go outside. Talking was banned except at certain times. Everything in a prisoner's cell had an assigned place, even the soap.

During the next two years, Alan questioned old-timers about previous escape attempts. There had been 10 attempts since the prison opened in 1934. Inmates had tied tin cans to their waists as floatation devices. They had disguised themselves as army officers. They had stormed guard towers, attacked guards, climbed the fence, and swam for the mainland. All efforts had failed.

But Alan was not discouraged. He just needed the perfect plan.

Before Alan could think of such a plan, he was transferred. He eventually wound up in federal prison in Atlanta, Georgia, where he became acquainted with three other inmates.

John and Clarence Anglin

John and Clarence Anglin were brothers who stole cars and robbed banks. Both had tried to escape from prison several times. A man named Frank Morris was also imprisoned in Atlanta. Age 32, Frank Morris had been incarcerated almost continually since he was 13.

He had escaped from a state prison in Louisiana only to be caught a year later when he committed another crime.

In June 1958, Alan was transferred back to Alcatraz, and by the spring of 1961, the Anglin brothers and Frank were there, too. They were four men with one thing on their minds—escape.

Alcatraz resembled an impenetrable fortress, but it was actually falling apart. The cell house was built in 1909. Because all freshwater had to be shipped in, toilets on the island were flushed with seawater. After many decades of this, the saltwater had eroded the building, causing pipes to break and concrete to crumble.

Alcatraz was the most expensive federal prison in the nation. Congress kept threatening to shut it down. Therefore, rather than ask for bigger budgets, prison wardens left critical repairs undone and staff vacancies unfilled. When Alan returned to the Rock, he noticed these weaknesses and thought about how he could exploit them.

Frank Morris had been on Alcatraz only a few days when Alan approached him.

"I know a way out of here," Alan said. "Through a vent in the ceiling."

There had once been eight exhaust blowers on top of the cell blocks. Metal ductwork ran from these large fans to the ceiling and blew air out a vent hood on the roof. Through the years, the blowers had been dismantled and the vents sealed with concrete. However, some inmates insisted one exhaust blower above B block was still hooked up to a ceiling vent.

Alan was assigned to cell B152, which was located on the outside of B block. The cell's front door faced the empty A block and its back wall butted up against a utility corridor. Cell B152 was also far from the desk at the west end of Broadway, where guards congregated. Even better, Alan discovered that, because of budget cuts, the warden had closed down the east gun gallery, so no observation deck overlooked Alan's end of the cell house. B152 was three tiers below the ceiling vent rumored to open onto the roof.

Alan was determined to get a look at that vent.

A painting job with the maintenance crew granted Alan the look he wanted. It also revealed more of Alcatraz's weaknesses. In the summer of 1961, Alan was ordered to paint the interior of the cell house. Every day, a guard escorted him to a cell, locked him in, and left Alan to work.

Alan noticed that the concrete underneath the paint was pockmarked with little holes. When Alan dug his fingernail into one of those holes, gravel and sand slid out. The walls were weak.

Then in July, a pipe burst. Water and toilet waste flooded the B block utility corridor. A guard locked Alan into the utility corridor and ordered him to clean up the mess.

Looking around, Alan realized he had hit the jackpot.

A maze of sturdy pipes and electrical wiring stretched from floor to ceiling—the perfect ladder to the cell house ceiling. Also, he discovered that the concrete in the wall was so spongy in some places that he could scrape it off. On the other side of this decaying wall was Alan's cell.

When Alan began painting the cell house ceiling, he used a three-story scaffold on wheels. From the top of the scaffolding, he could see above B block. The rumors were correct. An exhaust blower was still attached to a vent in the ceiling.

Alan West wanted co-conspirators. He told Clarence Anglin about his discoveries and Clarence told his brother. The men brainstormed escape ideas during meals and in the rec yard. An unspoken agreement was reached. Alan West, Frank Morris, and Clarence and John Anglin were going to break the Rock.

The men knew they needed to be close to each other for any plan to work, so they requested cell transfers. By September 1961, the men were in four adjacent cells at the east end of B block.

A chiseled air vent in one of the cells on
Alcatraz that led to the utility corridor

The first obstacle was breaking out of their cells. The back of each cell had a small air vent at the bottom of the wall. This 5-by-9-inch opening was covered by a diamond-patterned metal grill. Each man would remove his grill and widen the opening to create a doorway into the utility corridor. From there, they could climb up the pipes to the top of B block.

The problem was that to widen the hole, they had to break through five inches of concrete. Although corroded in spots, the concrete was still tough.

At 7:00 each evening, Happy Hour began. The normal no-talking rule was set aside for 60 minutes. Some men played chess. Others chatted with friends. Many prisoners played instruments.

The noise of guitars, horns, and accordions masked the sound of metal against concrete coming from the cells of Alan and the other men.

Soup spoons became their pickaxes. The men sharpened the ends of the spoons on rough edges of their concrete floors. During Happy Hour, they worked in shifts, two digging while the other two kept watch. The process was painfully slow. However, through the weeks, they managed to dig a series of small holes about three inches deep. They did not break all the way through into the utility corridor because that could be quickly spotted by a guard. The men pocketed the chunks of concrete and sand and emptied their pockets during rec time.

Every night, the men camouflaged the holes with paste made from bar soap and they painted it with green paint smuggled in by Alan. The men further disguised these holes by propping up instrument cases against the back wall or hanging raincoats or towels to strategically disguise their work.

But as the openings in the wall got bigger, so did the danger of discovery.

Every man on Alcatraz feared the cold, turbulent waters of the bay. Inmates had drowned trying to swim the 1¼ miles to San Francisco.

During their time in the rec yard, the Anglins, Frank Morris, and Alan West brainstormed how they could survive the long-distance swim. "Why don't we just build a raft?" Clarence suggested one day.

Alan considered this. He had heard of the two inmates who made water wings out of the rubbery material of a prison raincoat. The story did not have a happy ending. One of the inmates chickened out and the other one drowned. Still, paddling a raft was better than swimming.

All inmates were issued a long raincoat. Not only did it rain a lot on Alcatraz, but the island was also home to thousands of seagulls. The inmates joked that these birds had better aim than the guards. At the end of rec time, most inmates had at least one green-gray streak running down their raincoats. John worked in the laundry room, where raincoats were stored.

A raincoat raft would need to be inflated. Frank knew it would take too long to blow up a four-person raft by mouth, so he ordered a concertina. He dismantled the miniature accordion and turned its bellows into a hand pump the men could use to pump up the raft on escape night.

Alan called in favors from other inmates. One man designed a sketch of a life jacket made from raincoats that could be inflated with the dipstick from a spray bottle. Inmates in the glove factory sewed them.

Furniture repair workers slipped brass screws, nuts, and washers in their socks and slid short lengths of board down their shirts. Brass did not set off the alarms on Alcatraz's antiquated metal detectors.

At night, Alan kept one eye out for the guards while he sealed the life jackets with waterproof rubber adhesive and built two wooden paddles. He also concocted a plan to get access to the ceiling vent. He finished painting the entire ceiling of the cell house except for the section above B block.

When an inexperienced, young guard named John Herring came on duty, Alan approached him.

"I need to get up on the cell block to paint that last section," Alan said.

"I thought you had finished the job," Herring said.

"Just got that last bit," Alan replied.

Prison officials with more authority than Herring had ordered the cell house painted, so the officer saw nothing suspicious in Alan's request. He unlocked the door that led to the top of the cell block and gestured for Alan to enter.

"Watch yourself up there," he cautioned before locking Alan in and returning to the cell house floor.

While Alan worked, he took in every detail of the ceiling vent. That night, he reported what he saw to the others. As soon as they broke through their cell walls, they would climb the utility corridor pipes and tackle the vent.

The soap paste could no longer hide the gaping hole in John Anglin's wall so he made a duplicate grill. John removed the cardboard backing from a three-ring binder. He cut out hundreds of little diamond shapes to match the real grill and framed the cardboard with the wood. Then he painted it green. The fake grill fit perfectly into the hole in John's cell wall and could easily be popped in and out.

On April 25, 1962, the lieutenant in the cell house wrote "routine night" in his duty log. However, the night was anything but routine. As men snored around him, John knocked out the final piece of cement and squeezed through the hole in his cell wall. The stench of urine in the dark corridor made his eyes water.

John crawled to his brother's cell and knocked on his vent. When Clarence peered out, his grin stretched from ear to ear. While Clarence kept a lookout, John made another fake cover and disguised the hole on the wall of the utility corridor.

The next morning, when they learned John had broken out for a few hours, Alan and Frank panicked. Guards performed a bed check several times a night.

An empty bed would launch an immediate manhunt. But Clarence and John had solved this problem. They named their solution "Oink."

Oink was a fake human head made of wire covered in cement sludge. After it dried, the brothers painted the face a light pink color. Clarence used hair from his job in the prison barber shop to create eyebrows, eyelashes, and hair. Soon, Oink had three brothers. The fake heads would be used as decoys so the men could leave their cells at night.

One problem still remained. The vent above cell block B was visible to any guard strolling down Broadway. Alan came up with a bold solution to this final obstacle to escape.

Alcatraz was a spotless facility and the guards were fanatical about keeping it that way. One morning, before Alan began to paint, he swept dirt into a large mound and pushed the pile over the edge of the cell block. Dirt rained down on Broadway.

Lieutenant Ordway, a finicky officer, walked by. Alan heard dirt crunch under his shoes. Ordway did, too. He ordered Officer Herring to clean up the mess.

"You have to quit sweeping up there," Herring told Alan.

"But it's filthy," Alan said. "I can't paint over all this dirt."

Then he proposed a solution. "How about I hang some blankets from the ceiling? It'll stop the dirt from sailing over the edge."

Herring hesitated. He did not have the power to authorize such a move, but he told Alan he would get back to him. Permission was granted, and later that afternoon, Herring told the laundry department to send some blankets up to B block. Alan told John Anglin to stall on this order until the following day, when Herring would be not working.

Two days later, Herring returned from his day off to find 40 blankets strung from the ceiling to the top of B block. Alan had created a private room completely encircling the exhaust blower and ceiling vent.

"What in the world did you do?" Herring asked.

"This was how many blankets that laundry sent up," Alan said, "so I figured you wanted them all hung."

Lieutenant Ordway noticed the blankets and ordered them taken down immediately. Alan had expected this and was prepared.

"I did a lot of work putting this up!" he ranted to Herring. "Do you know how long it would take for me to remove them all?"

Alan knew how to exploit power struggles between the officers. He worked on Herring's ego. Ordway was not Herring's supervisor, was he? Who did Ordway think he was ordering Herring around?

Other prison officials got involved in the dispute and the blankets remained. Now the escape team had a place to hide their supplies, build their raft, and open up the ceiling vent.

———◆———

The pace of work escalated. Every night, John and Frank tucked their masks into bed and used the cover of Happy Hour to scramble to the top of the cell block. Clarence kept a lookout while Alan chipped away at his cell wall. He had not yet broken through.

John constructed the raft while Frank tackled the vent. The metal duct that led from the exhaust blower to the vent came off easily, but when Frank stuck his head into the shaft that led to the ceiling, his heart sank. An iron grate blocked the opening to the roof. Heavy brackets riveted it in place.

The ceiling shaft was only 18 inches wide, and Frank could not maneuver a saw in such a narrow space. The men rigged up an old hair clipper to make a drill, but that failed immediately. Frank tried hand tools next. The wrench was too cumbersome, so he set it on the exhaust blower and grabbed a screwdriver.

As sweat rolled down his temples and iron flakes fell into his eyes, Frank twisted and pried. Finally, he managed to wedge the screwdriver into a tiny gap between a rivet and the grate.

Just then, the whistle that signaled the end of music hour blew. Frank sighed in exhaustion and dropped his arm. It hit the side of the exhaust blower, knocking the wrench.

The tool fell off the cell block, clanging against the pipes as it plunged three stories. With a final thud, the wrench hit the floor of the utility corridor. For a moment, there was complete silence. Then the cell block exploded with noise. Men banged their cups against cell bars. They blared saxophones, slammed music cases, and shouted to each other. By this time, the escape was an open secret among inmates, who were coming to the aid of their prison brothers.

"Shut down that racket!" a guard shouted.

Frank scrambled down pipes and slipped into his cell. That had been a close call.

Time was running out. The guards were pressuring Alan to finish painting the ceiling. The blanket room would soon be ripped down. But Frank had still not been able to remove the rivets holding the ceiling grate in place.

The men worked feverishly during Happy Hour on June 10. Alan hammered hard on his cell wall. The Anglins completed the raincoat raft by gluing three side floaters together in a triangle shape. They had no way of knowing whether the raft would leak until they put it in the water on escape night.

Frank finally managed to insert a homemade saw blade between the rivets and the brackets. His neck muscles cramped and sweat rolled down his back as he worked the saw blade back and forth.

The whistle signaling the end of Happy Hour sounded and the Anglins returned to their cells, but Frank kept sawing. Finally, at 3:30 the next morning, he removed the final rivet. Behind this was a piece of sheet metal designed to keep out birds and rain. Frank easily unscrewed this with his fingers. The cool night breeze wafted down onto his face. Freedom was so close.

By 4 a.m. all supplies had been stashed in the exhaust blower, and the men were asleep in their beds. Would this be their last night in Alcatraz?

The night of June 11, 1962, the sky was clear and a cool, light wind blew. A half-moon lit the sky above San Francisco Bay. As soon as the guard passed his cell for the 8 p.m. count, Frank slipped through the hole in his wall. He retrieved the masks from above and returned to the utility corridor.

The Anglin brothers waited at their cell openings. Frank handed them their masks and set Oink on the floor outside Alan's cell.

"I should have the vent completely open by 9:30," he whispered to Alan through the partial opening in Alan's wall. It was still not wide enough for Alan to crawl through. Alan nodded and chipped faster.

At 9:22, Clarence appeared outside Alan's cell. "We can see the moon."

Alan pushed frantically at his wall. Clarence tried to push from the other side. The wall did not budge.

"Get Frank and tell him to bring down a pipe," Alan ordered.

Frank appeared a few seconds later and passed a metal pipe to Alan. Both men tried to break through, but the wall remained solid. Frank shifted from foot to foot.

"You can't leave me," Alan said.

The Anglin brothers were alone on the top of the cell block, and Frank did not trust them. "They'll leave without us," Frank said.

"Get Clarence," Alan ordered. "All three of us will be able to break through this."

Frank said he'd be right back.

Alan West never saw Frank Morris again.

———◆———

No one knows exactly what transpired on top of the cell block that night. However, information gathered in the following days suggest this story.

Around 10:30 that night, something hit the roof with a thunderous crash that echoed throughout the cell house. Officer Young reported the sound to Lieutenant Weir, who was working in the control room. The crash came from a vent hood on the roof. When Frank lifted it from inside the ceiling shaft, the wind must have yanked the hood from his hands and slammed it against the roof. Fear of discovery probably catapulted the Anglins and Frank out of the ceiling shaft. One of them dropped a paddle and did not stop to pick it up.

The men slid to the ground on a 45-foot exhaust pipe. One of the iron rods securing the pipe bent under their weight, and the pipe banged loudly against the side of the building.

Officer Young heard this clang, too. He reported to Lieutenant Weir that a second sound had come from the direction of the prison hospital. Weir went to investigate. The prison was short-staffed that night, so no officer was available to patrol the grounds.

If a guard had gone outside, he would have seen Frank and the Anglins scramble over the fence surrounding the rec yard and leap to a hill below. They ran along the base of the water tower and down a rocky cliff. The trio left a trail of broken brush.

Inside the Officer's Club, off-duty prison guards were bowling and socializing. They were enjoying themselves so much no one noticed three shadowy figures dart past the building.

The escapees ran down another hill and, suddenly, there in front of them was San Francisco Bay. They must have unfolded the raft, and Frank hooked up his concertina bellows and began to pump.

Back inside the prison, Lieutenant Weir investigated the hospital carefully. Finding nothing unusual, he returned to the cell house. Officer Young said there had not been any more strange noises. The rest of the shift passed without incident.

The waves of San Francisco Bay crashed against the rocks as Frank Morris and the Anglin brothers tied on their life jackets and eased the raft into the water. They climbed aboard and one of the men picked up the paddle and rowed furiously for land.

No one knows what happened next. Frank Morris and Clarence and John Anglin were never seen again.

Alan West finally broke through his cell wall at about 2 a.m. Oink lay on the floor in the corridor, but Alan ignored him. The mask was no use now. Alan climbed to the roof. Before him were the star-studded sky and an empty black sea. Alan returned to his bed.

Inmates in nearby cells heard him crying.

Prison officials discovered the escape the next morning. Alan West told the authorities everything he knew. The FBI, Coast Guard, and the Army joined the search for the escaped convicts.

In the following days, clues washed up. A paddle was found floating in the waters close to nearby Angel Island, but a search of the island turned up nothing. A bag made of raincoat material was fished out of the ocean. It contained photographs of relatives of the Anglins and a list of people to contact. A homemade life jacket was found on a beach three miles north of the Golden Gate Bridge. However, no bodies were ever found.

Alcatraz was permanently closed in 1963. Alan West served the rest of his sentence elsewhere and was released in 1967. However, he was quickly arrested again for robbery. Alan died in prison on December 21, 1978.

Other inmates at Alcatraz believed Alan West could have broken through his cell wall if he wanted to. Why he would choose not to run is a mystery. Perhaps it was fear of the chilly grip of the Pacific currents. Or maybe Alan wanted someone to remain behind to tell the story of the men who finally broke the Rock.

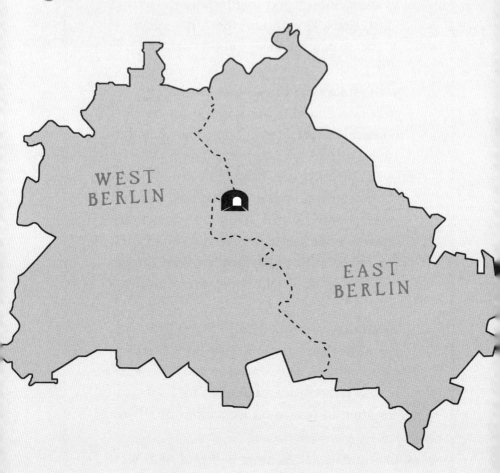

GERMANY

-------- the Berlin Wall
dividing East
and West Berlin

WEST
BERLIN

EAST
BERLIN

 1962
Residents of
West Berlin dig
a tunnel to help
residents of
East Berlin escape.

YOU
ARE
HERE

1945
World War II
ends

1961
The Berlin Wall
divides East Berlin
from West Berlin

1989
The Berlin Wall
is torn down

Chapter Five

Tunnel 29

The night of August 13, 1961, the citizens
of East Berlin, Germany, were trapped as
they slept. Soldiers unrolled massive spools
of barbed wire along the 28-mile border
between East Berlin and West Berlin.

When the sun rose, a man named Peter Schmidt woke
to a changed world. East German guards manned
checkpoints along the border. Peter was studying art
at a college in West Berlin, but lived with his family
in East Berlin. Now, he and thousands of other East
German students were forbidden from crossing the
border to attend class.

Overnight, East Berliners lost their jobs in West
Berlin because they could not get to work. Parents
were cut off from children, husbands separated from
wives, and friends severed from friends.

Two Italian college students, Luigi "Gigi" Spina and Domenico "Mimmo" Sesta, were Peter's close friends. They lived in West Berlin, but their Italian passports allowed them to cross the border. A week after the border was sealed, Gigi and Mimmo visited Peter.

"You must make a run for it," Mimmo urged.

But Peter had seen what happened to people who tried to flee west. Some jumped from buildings along the border, only to die in the fall. Others were shot while dashing through barbed wire or swimming across a canal. Peter had a wife, infant daughter, and elderly mother to consider.

Building the Berlin Wall in 1961

"I cannot leave my family," he said. "Besides, the wall won't last." Many East Germans believed the barrier was temporary. They were wrong.

❖

Berlin had been one city until 1945. When Nazi Germany was defeated in World War II, the Allies (United States, Soviet Union, France, and Great Britain) divided the country into four occupation zones. Germany's capital city of Berlin was also divided into four sections, but the city itself lay within the Soviet occupation zone. The Allies planned to rebuild the bombed-out country and then hold democratic elections for a new German government.

However, tensions between the United States and the Soviet Union escalated into the Cold War.

This war of words and ideas, which would last 45 years, was caused by a clash of opposing cultures. The United States was a democracy where people had the right to vote and speak freely. The Soviet Union had a totalitarian government controlled by the communist party. Citizens could not vote and they could not criticize the government.

The economic systems of the two countries were at odds, too. The United States believed in capitalism. In this system, people are free to own their own businesses, and their income depends on their work. In contrast, the Soviet Union had a socialist economy. The government owned the farms, factories, and businesses, and the wealth of the country was supposed to be divided equally between everyone.

After World War II, the Soviet Union propped up communist governments throughout Eastern Europe.

When the other Allies combined their zones of West Berlin and developed a strong, capitalist economy there, the Soviets set up a communist government in its own zone. By 1949, Germany had become two countries—West Germany, which was democratic and capitalist, and East Germany, which was totalitarian and communist. East Berlin was part of East Germany and West Berlin belonged to West Germany.

West Germany's economy grew richer while East Germany's stalled. Although no elections were held in East Germany, citizens voted with their feet by crossing the border into West Berlin and never returning. By 1961, 3 million East Germans had fled to the West through West Berlin. The East German government got permission from its protector, the Soviet Union, to plug this leak with a wall.

From the moment the first brick of the Berlin Wall was laid, East Germans looked for ways to escape.

Peter Schmidt soon realized life would not return to normal. The barbed wire became a concrete wall 13 feet tall that eventually encircled the entire city of West Berlin, a distance of 100 miles. The barren strip of land bordering the wall was called "the death strip."

Watching from 300 towers, East German guards shot anyone in this zone. Barbed wire was laid in canals and land mines were buried along the death strip. Government spies were planted in apartment buildings, schools, hospitals, and offices. These informants were the eyes and ears of the Stasi, which was East Germany's secret police. The lack of freedom was suffocating.

When Mimmo and Gigi visited him in February 1962, Peter begged his friends, "I can't take it anymore. Can you help my family escape?"

The Italians agreed, but it would not be easy. With a baby and an elderly mother, the Schmidts could not go over the wall.

They would have to go under it.

Back in West Berlin, Mimmo and Gigi recruited their friend, Wolfhardt Schroedter. He was an advanced engineering student who had fled East Germany four years earlier. The men's first task was to find a tunnel route. The entrance and exits needed to be hidden and not too far apart. The soil needed to be sandy enough to dig in, but not so loose it would collapse.

They located a cellar in an apartment near the wall in East Berlin. After several days of scouting, the men found an old factory close to the border in West Berlin. Although half the building had been bombed during World War II, the half not in ruins was being used to manufacture the swizzle sticks used in cocktail drinks. The factory had a large cellar with several rooms and a secluded courtyard.

The Italians approached the owner and asked if they could rent the basement and first floor for their band to rehearse in. The owner rolled his eyes. "Do not tell me such stories. You are going to dig a tunnel," he said. This man had fled East Germany and had no fondness for communism. He let the Italians use the space rent-free.

On May 9, 1962, Gigi, Mimmo, and Wolfhardt used a pickax to open a hole in the cellar of the swizzle-stick factory. For three nights, the men dug a 15-foot shaft. They were sweaty and muddy. Their shoulders ached and their hands were callused. But they were also excited. It was time to plan the tunnel's design.

An old map from the city works department served as a guide to what lay under the streets of Berlin. The tunnel had to be deep enough to avoid the maze of underground water pipes and street-car wires. Wolfhardt, the engineer, did the calculations. The tunnel had to be about 20 feet deep and stretch for 400 feet. Most of this would be under East Berlin.

Digging such a tunnel would take months. There was no time to lose. Peter Schmidt had received orders to report for duty with the East German army at the end of 1962. If he did not escape soon, he would be sent far from the help of his friends.

They needed more diggers and needed them fast.

———◆———

The college campus was a ripe recruiting ground. More than 30 men helped dig off and on, but the core team was made up of men motivated by personal reasons.

Ulrich Pfeifer, for example, was a construction engineer. He had fled East Berlin through the sewers, but his girlfriend was caught and sentenced to seven years in prison. Hasso Herschel had been a political prisoner in East Germany and was determined to help his sister escape. Joachim Neumann, also an engineering student, had a girlfriend stuck in East Berlin. Joachim Rudolph and Manfred Krebs were friends of Wolfhardt and, like him, they had fled the East and wanted to help others escape.

The crew worked around the clock in eight-hour shifts. Only one man could dig at a time. He had to lay on his back and push the spade with his feet. Then, the digger had to twist his body around to dump the shovel full of dirt into a small cart. It was a slow process.

The air underground was only 55 degrees. It smelled unlike anything the men had ever smelled before. Damp, musty, and loamy—the odor of undisturbed centuries.

Sounds from aboveground were muted. Street cars rumbled. Manhole covers clanged. The footsteps of a man clomped, while those of a woman tapped.

By June 6, 1962, the diggers had reached the death zone. East German police had been known to press listening devices to the ground. If they heard suspicious activity, they might dig a hole and set off a charge of dynamite.

Little by little, the crew innovated to make their work easier. They laid sheets of wood on the dirt floor with a steel rail down the center to build a mini-railroad track. Attaching wheels to the bottom of the cart turned it into a mini train car. The men hooked an electrified winch and rope to the cart. When the cart was full of dirt, a man positioned at the entrance of the tunnel pushed a button to pull the cart back up the track.

The crew ran a telephone wire down the length of the tunnel so the diggers could communicate. They also sawed 20 tons of lumber into short beams to prop up the tunnel's walls and ceiling.

Gigi lit matches frequently to test how much oxygen was in the air. On the day the flame flickered and went out, the men knew they needed more air in the tunnel. Dozens of stove pipes were taped together to create an air shaft. The motors of vacuum cleaners became fans. One day, someone drizzled perfume into the air shaft, and another day, someone dumped in some cognac. The digging seemed easier when the air smelled good.

The seven rooms in the cellar slowly filled up. Dirt piled up in the courtyard. Progress was steady. Then, disaster struck.

A drip in the ceiling became a leak. Soon, four inches of water pooled on the tunnel floor. Sections of the wall and ceiling collapsed. Clay turned the consistency of greasy, brown butter. The men feared they would have to abandon the project.

The diggers used a hand pump to drain the water but that was like bailing the ocean with a teaspoon. In one week, the men pumped 8,000 gallons out of the tunnel. Mimmo and Gigi decided to convince West Berlin city officials to dig up the street and fix what must be a leaky water pipe.

But this meant revealing their secret operation.

The official policy of the West German government, backed by the United States, was not to interfere with the Berlin Wall. As long as the freedom of West Berlin was respected, the communists could govern their citizens the way they wanted. However, the *unofficial* policy of West Berlin's government was to aid people helping others to escape. A few days after Mimmo and Gigi met with a government official, the leak stopped. Relief.

As the diggers waited for the tunnel to dry out, the situation aboveground was reaching a boiling point.

◆

August 13, 1962, was a somber day. The Berlin Wall was one year old. At noon, West Berliners observed a minute of silence. Factory machinery was turned off. Cars, buses and trains stopped. The silence was deafening.

When the minute ended, West Berlin exploded in protest. A two-mile line of cars drove slowly past the wall, the drivers pressing on their horns. Protestors erected a huge cross on the western side of the wall with the words "We Accuse" printed across it. West Berliners stormed a bridge into East Berlin and others attacked the wall itself.

When West German police pushed them back from the border, the protestors threw stones and hurled insults. While the West screamed in protest, the East hunkered down in silent terror.

On August 17, a tragedy aboveground spurred the digging crew to work faster. Peter Fechter, an 18-year-old bricklayer, was shot trying to escape. The boy lay bleeding less than a foot from the wall on the East Berlin side.

The East German guards seemed paralyzed, their guns sighted on the boy who lay moaning as blood pooled under his body. West Berlin police watched, but the law prohibited them from crossing the border.

"Help me!" Fechter cried. "Why aren't you helping me?"

One West German police officer threw a roll of bandages over the wall, but Fechter was too weak to help himself. He curled into a fetal position and his cries became quieter.

Hundreds of West Berliners gathered along the wall and shouted at the East German guards, "You criminals! You murderers!"

Finally, four East German guards hauled him away. That evening, a sign went up in a window in East Berlin: "He is dead."

West Berlin ignited in anger. All night long, thousands of people hurled stones, bottles, and iron bars at the East German border police. When U.S. military trucks drove up to help the West German police restore order, the crowd turned on the Americans with cries of "Yankee cowards! Traitors! Yankees go home!"

The diggers hung a photograph of Peter Fechter inside the tunnel. They were more determined than ever to bring their friends and family members to freedom. But then the tunnel sprang another leak.

The crew needed three more weeks of around-the-clock digging before they would reach the exit in the apartment cellar they had chosen months earlier. They dug faster, but the leak grew bigger. There was a broken water pipe somewhere, but now the tunnel was under East Berlin. The only solution was to find a closer exit and move up the escape date.

Their city map showed an apartment that appeared to be directly above where their tunnel currently ended, at 7 Schönholzer Strasse, one block back from the wall. Mimmo crossed the border to do a quick surveillance. He peered through a window into the building's lobby. The room had two doors. One must lead to a basement. But what was in that basement and what kind of flooring would the diggers have to break through? The escape would be much more risky if they had to break into a building the crew knew so little about. But the tunnel floor had become a river of mud.

It was now or never.

The escape date was bumped up to September 14. The team needed a courier. This person would cross into East Berlin on escape day. Armed with coded messages, the courier's job was to let the refugees know what time to arrive at the tunnel's entrance. One wrong move would alert the Stasi.

Mimmo's fiancée, Ellen Schau, arrived in West Berlin on September 10 to celebrate her 22nd birthday, which happened to fall on September 14. Ellen always dressed in elegant clothes and wore her red hair up in a chic French twist. No one would mistake her for a secret agent.

When Mimmo picked up Ellen from the airport, he proposed an unusual birthday celebration. Would she go under cover into East Berlin? Ellen had never been to East Berlin and did not know the city. If she lost her way, the entire escape plan would fall apart. Ellen was terrified, but she said yes.

The diggers rented an apartment in West Berlin with a window overlooking Schönholzer Strasse. On escape day, one of the crew would keep watch on building number 7. The team worked out a code to alert Ellen to danger. If a white sheet was hanging out the apartment window, the coast was clear. A red sheet meant abort the mission immediately.

The countdown began.

On September 11, Ellen memorized East Berlin maps, rendezvous locations, and codes.

On September 12, Mimmo crossed into East Berlin to tell Peter Schmidt the escape date had been moved up.

On September 13, the team went over assignments for the next day. Some men would be lookouts in the apartment overlooking the wall. Others would be stationed inside the tunnel to aid refugees as they crawled to safety. Joachim Rudolph, Hasso Herschel, Joachim Neumann, and Gigi Spina would break through the cellar floor of 7 Schönholzer Strasse and guide the refugees into the tunnel. These men would be armed. Just in case.

September 14 dawned warm and sunny. Ellen crossed into East Berlin without a hitch and took a taxi to a church near the wall. In her purse, Ellen carried her passport, the list of codes, and money. Outside the church, Ellen glanced over the wall. A white sheet flapped from the window of the rented apartment.

The Schmidt family rose early. Peter's wife, Eveline, put on a new dress bought for this special day. Peter was more practical. He dressed in layers of underwear. If he was arrested, Peter knew he would wind up in a Stasi dungeon and he wanted to be warm.

The diggers took their positions. The advance team crawled through the tunnel, in water up to their ankles. When they reached the end, everyone listened intently. All was silent above them.

Hasso Herschel climbed up on another man's shoulders. He pushed the tip of a screwdriver into the ground above his head. It went through easily, and the men sighed in relief. The basement floor was dirt, not concrete. But when Herschel removed the screwdriver, water sprayed out of the hole. The diggers looked at each other in alarm. The Stasi had been known to flood tunnels. The entire basement above them might be filled with water.

There was only one way to find out.

Herschel chipped at the hole. The water remained a tiny sprinkle. It was only a leaky pipe and posed no danger. He thrust a mirror up into the cellar and rotated his hand to survey the surroundings. The room was empty.

The men climbed out, treading as softly as possible. There was a critical detail they had to check. Were they actually in the basement of 7 Schönholzer Strasse? Joachim Rudolph volunteered to go outside and check. He put on workman's coveralls. If anyone questioned him, Rudolph would claim to be fixing an electrical problem.

Rudolph climbed the cellar steps and entered the lobby. It was empty. He opened the front door and stepped outside. Barbed wire ran down the center of the street and armed guards manned checkpoints at each end. Rudolph tried to appear casual as he strolled a few steps down the sidewalk and glanced back at the building.

A white enamel sign hung above the door with the address in bold, black print—7 Schönholzer Strasse. Rudolph sighed in relief. The diggers had come up in the right building. He returned to the cellar and reported the good news.

As the advance crew waited for the refugees, the lobby above began to bustle with activity. People were returning home from work. The diggers listened to the tenants laugh and chatter. Joachim Rudolph wondered what would happen if the first wave of refugees arrived when the lobby was full of people.

Peter Schmidt and his family arrived at a tavern a few blocks from Schönholzer Strasse. Another family of refugees, Hasso Herschel's sister and her family, entered the bar a few minutes later. Everyone tried to act normal, but their eyes darted to the door every time it opened as they watched for the courier.

The bar began to fill with East Berliners who had just finished work. The refugees did not fit in. Herschel's sister was wearing her black, designer wedding dress and high heels, and Peter Schmidt's mother was an old woman. Both couples had restless toddlers.

Suddenly, Ellen entered the bar, a folded newspaper clutched to her side. The refugees stiffened. They had been told to watch for a woman with a newspaper folded under her arm.

Ellen had never gone to a bar by herself before. She felt like she had a target on her back as she walked to the counter and bought a box of matches. She glanced around the bar and immediately spotted the refugees. They sat rigid, eyes glued to the matches in Ellen's hand. That was the second code they had been told to watch for. Ellen had done her job. The refugees knew it was time for them to go to the tunnel. Ellen strolled out of the bar, heading for her next rendezvous.

The Schmidts left the tavern immediately, and the other family followed 15 minutes later, as they had been instructed. When the Schmidts arrived at 7 Schönholzer Strasse, the lobby was empty.

"Now what?" Eveline Schmidt thought. Then she spotted a door at the end of the lobby.

Just inside that door on the basement steps, the diggers waited with their guns ready. The refugees had been given a password to identify themselves. The secret word was "potemkin," which means fake.

Suddenly, the cellar door swung open. The men raised their weapons, fingers on the triggers.

Eveline was so nervous she forgot to give the password before yanking open the cellar door. In front of her stood a group of men, their guns pointing at her head. That moment seemed to last forever as terror paralyzed Eveline. Had her family just walked into a Stasi trap?

Then Gigi Spina pushed past the other diggers and swept Peter Schmidt up in a hug. Without another word, the diggers led the refugees down the tunnel shaft.

Eveline crawled on hands and knees. Peter was right behind her, followed by his mother. Their toddler was passed from person to person. The little girl did not even whimper.

Back in the factory basement in West Berlin, one of the crew waited at the top of the tunnel shaft. He heard a faint commotion below. Suddenly, a woman's arm popped out of the shaft, a purse in her hand.

A crown of messy hair appeared next. Then Eveline Schmidt came into view. Her new dress was covered in mud.

Mimmo emerged from the shaft, the Schmidt's toddler in his arms. Peter Schmidt's mother climbed out next, followed by her son. When Peter stepped out of the hole, he hoisted Mimmo off the floor in a huge embrace. The Schmidt family was finally free.

Late into the night, East Germans crawled under the Berlin Wall. The following day, a few more people came. By the evening of September 15, the rescuers had to abandon operations because there were 12 inches of water in the tunnel. Twenty-nine people escaped to freedom on this subterranean road of mud, which ever after was known as Tunnel 29.

> The Cold War ended in the fall of 1989 as relations between the Soviet Union and the United States thawed and improved. The night of November 9, 1989, the border between East and West Berlin was opened. Tens of thousands of Germans passed through checkpoints freely. People climbed on top of the wall and drank champagne. Fireworks lit up the night. For the first time in 28 years, there was no East and West. There was only Berlin.
>
> During the following months, the wall was torn down, and Germany was finally reunited on October 3, 1990.

The fall of the Berlin Wall
photo credit: Daniel Antal

abolitionist: someone who wanted to end slavery.

abyss: a deep gorge.

activist: a person who fights for something they believe in.

Allies: the countries that fought against Germany in World War II. The major Allied powers included the United States, the Soviet Union, France and Great Britain.

Antarctica: the continent around the South Pole.

antiquated: old-fashioned.

apprehend: to catch someone.

apprentice: a person who learns a job or skill by working for someone who is good at it.

assassinate: to murder an important person for political or religious reasons.

auction: a public sale in which goods or property are sold to the highest bidder.

auctioneer: a person who conducts auctions by accepting bids and declaring goods sold.

bid: an offer for something, especially at an auction.

biracial: having parents from two races.

bloodhound: a large dog with a very keen sense of smell, used in tracking.

brand: a mark burned into skin by a hot metal tool. The mark shows ownership.

budget: a certain amount of money for a company or organization to spend in a specific time.

cairn: a mound of stones or snow built as a landmark.

capitalism: an economic system in which a country's trade and industry are controlled by private individuals and operated for profit.

cattle car: a train car used to transport cattle.

chasm: a deep crack or hole.

checkpoint: a barrier along a border where travelers must go through security checks.

citizen: a person who legally belongs to a country and has the rights and protection of that country.

civilized: describes a community of people with a highly developed culture and social organization.

Cold War: a rivalry between the Soviet Union and the United States that began after World War II.

collaborator: a person who works with others. During war, it means a person who works with the enemy.

colossal: very large.

communist: a political system controlled by a single party that believes the wealth of the country should be owned by everyone and shared evenly.

concentration camp: during WWII, large camps where Jews and other minorities were imprisoned by the Nazis and forced to perform hard labor or exterminated.

continent: one of Earth's largest land areas.

courier: a messenger.

crevasse: a wide, deep break or opening in a shelf of ice or the earth.

debt: an amount of money or something else that is owed.

decoy: to lure or entice someone into a trap.

Deep South: a region of the southeastern United States that includes the states of Alabama, Georgia, Louisiana, Mississippi, North Carolina, and South Carolina.

democracy: a system of government where the people choose who will represent and govern them.

democratic: supporting democracy and its principles of freedom.

deport: to expel a person or group of people from a country.

desert: an ecosystem that lacks water, receiving 10 inches or less of precipitation each year.

disguise: a way of changing one's appearance or concealing one's identity.

disobedient: refusing to obey.

document: to record in writing or in photography.

double agent: an agent who pretends to act as a spy for one side while spying for the enemy.

duct: a channel or tube for conveying something.

economic: having to do with the resources and wealth of a country.

erode: to gradually wear away.

ethnic: sharing customs, languages, and beliefs.

excursion: a short journey or trip.

execute: to carry out a sentence of death.

expedition: a trip taken by a group of people for a specific purpose, such as exploration, scientific research, or war.

exploit: to take full advantage of something.

exterminate: to destroy completely or get rid of.

fertile: good for growing plants.

fidelity: loyalty.

Final Solution: the Nazi policy during World War II to exterminate all the Jews of Europe.

forge: to create a false document with the intent to defraud.

foolhardy: reckless.

freedom: the ability to choose and act without constraints.

frostbite: injury to body tissues caused by extreme cold.

fugitive: a person who has escaped.

genocide: the deliberate killing of a large group of people from a specific nation or ethnic group.

geologist: a scientist who studies rocks and soil in order to understand the history of the earth.

Gestapo: the secret police of Nazi Germany.

glacier: a slow-moving mass of ice.

hallucination: seeing, hearing, or smelling something that seems real but does not exist.

Hitler: Adolf Hitler was the chancellor of Germany from 1933 to 1945.

Holocaust: the murder of at least 6 million Jews and millions of other persecuted groups by Nazi Germany during World War II.

homosexual: a person who is sexually attracted to others of the same gender.

humiliation: extreme embarrassment.

husky: a powerful dog used to pull sleds.

impenetrable: impossible to pass through.

incarceration: being imprisoned.

ingenious: very clever and inventive.

inmate: a person confined to a prison.

innovate: to create something new or different.

invalid: a person made weak or disabled by illness or injury.

Jew: a person who is Jewish, who practices the religion of Judaism.

justice: fair action or treatment based on the law.

laborer: someone who does physical work using his or her hands.

lanolin: a fatty substance found naturally on sheep's wool.

liberty: freedom, the ability to act or live freely as one chooses.

lice: a small, wingless, parasitic insect that lives on the skin of mammals and birds.

maim: to injure a person so badly that part of their body no longer works.

mammoth: huge.

military: the army, navy, air force, and other armed services that protect a country and fight in wars.

navigate: to find your way from one place to another.

Nazi: a member of the National Socialist German Workers' Party before and during WWII.

nutrients: substances in food and soil that living things need to live and grow.

pack ice: large pieces of floating ice.

pallet: a cushioned sleeping surface.

partisan: a member of an armed group formed to fight secretly against an occupying force.

pemmican: a food made from dried meat, berries, and animal fat.

penitentiary: a prison.

perilous: full of danger or risk.

plantation: a large farm, usually where one crop is grown.

political: relating to running a government and holding onto power.

poultice: a soft, heated substance spread on a cloth and applied to the body to treat injury or illness.

precipitation: falling moisture in the form of rain, sleet, snow, and hail.

privileged: having rights or benefits that are given to only some people.

profit: the extra money or goods kept after paying costs of doing business.

providence: the protective care of God or nature.

ration: a fixed amount of something, such as food.

refugee: a person who has been forced to leave his country to avoid war, persecution, or natural disaster.

rendezvous: a meeting at an agreed time and place.

resistance: a force that opposes or slows down another force.

rheumatism: pain or stiffness of the back, arms, and legs.

Romani: a group of traditionally nomad people, often called gypsies.

runaway: a term used to describe a slave who escaped.

sabotage: to deliberately destroy, damage, or obstruct something for political or military purposes.

sanctuary: a place of safety.

Glossary

slavery: when slaves are used as workers. A slave is a person owned by another person and forced to work, without pay, against their will.

sledge: a large sled pulled by animals over snow or ice or over logs.

smuggle: to move goods illegally in or out of a country.

socialism: an economic system in which the production and distribution of goods is controlled by the government rather than private individuals.

Southern Hemisphere: the half of the planet south of the equator.

SS: short for Schutzstaffel, an elite group of German soldiers during World War II.

survey: to measure land areas to set up boundaries.

sustenance: something, especially food, that supports life or health.

swamp: an area of wet, spongy ground that grows woody plants such as trees and shrubs.

symbolize: to represent something by use of symbols.

terrain: land or ground and all of its physical features, such as hills, rocks, and water.

territory: an area of land.

tomb: a room or place where a dead person is buried.

totalitarian: a system of government that has absolute control over its people and requires them to be completely obedient.

transit camp: a place to temporarily house large groups of people that are being moved from one place to another.

Underground Railroad: a secret network of routes and safe houses used by abolitionists to guide runaway slaves to freedom.

unfaithfulness: the act of not being loyal or devoted.

villain: a character who does bad things.

wares: things for sale.

wharf: a pier where ships are loaded and unloaded.

winch: a machine used to haul or lift something heavy.

Resources

Books

Bitton-Jackson, Livia. *I Have Lived a Thousand Years: Growing Up in the Holocaust.* Simon Pulse, 1999.

Bredeson, Carmen. *After the Last Dog Died: The True-Life, Hair-Raising Adventure of Douglas Mawson's 1912 Antarctic Expedition.* National Geographic, 2003.

Bruce, J. Campbell. *Escape from Alcatraz: The True Crime Classic.* Ten Speed Press, 2005.

Hale, Nathan. *The Underground Abductor: An Abolitionist Tale about Harriet Tubman.* New York: Harry Abrams, 2015.

Lester, Julius. *From Slave Ship to Freedom Road.* Puffin Books, 1999.

Sis, Peter. *The Wall: Growing Up Behind the Iron Curtain.* New York: Farrar, Straus and Giroux, 2014.

Websites

Canadian Broadcasting Corporation has an interactive website that explores the Berlin Wall.
cbc.ca/passionateeye/blog/berlin-wall-interactive

From the safety of your living room, explore the frozen world of Antarctica with Discovering Antarctica.
discoveringantarctica.org.uk

Mission U.S. is an interactive game in which the reader becomes a 14-year-old Kentucky slave girl trying to escape.
mission-us.org

The United States Holocaust Memorial Museum is a memorial to the Holocaust that inspires citizens and leaders worldwide to confront hatred, prevent genocide, and promote human dignity. It offers online activities and learning materials for students.
ushmm.org

Smithsonian National Museum of African American History and Culture in Washington, DC, documents African American life, history, and culture.
nmaahc.si.edu